Table of Contents

Table of Authorities

Appellants Brief

Introduction

A case was initiated in the New York Supreme Court Albany County seeking to invalidate the New York State Board of Elections. It also sought to place candidates on the ballot after they had been deemed to have insufficient signatures by the New York State Board of Elections.

This action was appealed to the New York State Appellate Division Third Department. Then an appeal was made to the New York Court of Appeals which did not hear the case.

Thereafter, this case was brought to the United States District Court in Albany by voters whose constitutional election rights were denied to have their candidates on the ballot and by aggrieved candidates who were petitioners, as they are here.

Questions Presented

Does the New York State Board of Elections violate the United States Constitution and thus should be found unconstitutional and abolished and disbanded as it is presently constituted and a new election held with all candidates restored to the ballot?

Statement of the Case

The plaintiff-appellants are candidates for office or else are voters who support these candidates, who signed their petitions and want to vote for them for election. The candidates were on the ballot since July 8, 2014 but were thrown off at a meeting by the New York State Board of Elections on August 1, 2014.

In the current election year, the state and county boards of elections have become more aggressive than in past years of knocking candidates off the ballot. More than three hundred candidates have been thrown off the ballot, including state-wide candidates and candidates for US Congress and for State Senate and State Assembly. In most of these cases, this left only one candidate on the ballot, usually the incumbent, and therefore no election was held. The state courts have had to rule on these cases and have made many conflicting decisions. In one instance, the Supreme Court Appellate Division First Department in the Flacks case ruled that technical defects in the cover sheets are to be ignored. However, on the very same day, the Appellate Division Second Department ruled that technical defects no matter how minor are fatal and no opportunity for amendment is to be given.

Matter of Flacks v Board of Elections in The City of New York , 2013 NY Slip Op 05713 Decided on August 14, 2013

Matter of Gangemi v Board of Elections in the City of New York 2013 NY Slip Op 51368(U) Decided on August 8, 2013 Supreme Court, Kings County

The losing parties in these appeals thereafter requested the New York Court of Appeals for leave to appeal. However, for the last several years the New York Court of Appeals has denied all letter motions for leave to appeal, including these appeals, and therefore this conflicting menagerie of decisions has been left unresolved.

An authoritative work, **Goldfeder's Modern Election Law -- Third Edition** cites more than 240 reported decisions in which a ruling by the New York Boards of Election has been overturned by the New York Supreme Court or in which a decision by the New York Supreme Court has been reversed by the New York Appellate Division. See for example, Popkin v. Umane, 801 N.Y.S.2d 774 (2d Dept 2005). This is only a fraction of the number of cases decided as in most cases there has been no opinion and thus the decision was not reported.

The **ELECTION COMMISSIONER'S ASSOCIATION OF THE STATE OF NEW YORK** has put out a booklet entitled **BOARD OF ELECTIONS & PETITIONS: HOW TO SURVIVE A FEDERAL COURT CHALLENGE** *MATERIALS FOR THE PRESENTATION* **by STEVEN H. RICHMAN** General Counsel Board of Elections in the City of New York. This booklet provides traps and tricks to help the Commissioners and the candidates they favor prevent their rulings from being overturned by the courts.

What makes the instant case different from other cases is no objections were filed against the candidate for Governor, Sam Sloan, or the candidate for Lieutenant Governor, Nenad Bach. It has always been the rule and the law that where no objections are filed, the candidate remains on the ballot. Also, if there are objections, the objections must be specific, then the matter is referred to a clerk, a clerk's report is issued, and there is a hearing scheduled and held where the candidate or his counsel can appear and contest the clerk's report. The board makes a decision and then if the decision is adverse the candidate has three days to file a case in Supreme Court. The Supreme Court usually appoints a referee who rules on the objections.

None of this procedure was followed here. Instead, the candidates were just thrown off the ballot without any notice or opportunity for a hearing. This violated the principles set forth in Rivera-Powell v. N.Y.C. Bd. of Elections, 470 F.3d 458 (2d Cir. 2006) which held that there must be a pre-hearing or post-hearing procedure to challenge the deprivation of a right such as the right to appear on the ballot. In the case presented here there was no hearing at all. The candidates were just notified several days after a meeting, not a hearing, that was held on August 1, 2014 in which these four candidates had been thrown off the ballot. The fact is that there were no objections to Sam Sloan for Governor and Nenad Bach for Lieutenant Governor. Thus, under Election Law and especially under Section 6-154, the Board of Elections had no jurisdiction to remove these candidates from the ballot.

Sam Sloan is an internationally known and world-renowned chess player, well known to the 600,000 rated tournament chess players in the USA. His name is a household word among those voters. He is also an author and the publisher of more than 560 books and thus is a credible candidate.

In a normal case the issue becomes moot once the election was held. However, here in view of the outrageous and illegal acts and constitutional violations by the Boards of Elections, this court should act promptly to have a new election held and restore all the more than 300 candidates who were knocked off the ballot by the state and county boards of election's illegal and unconstitutional actions. The Boards of Elections themselves should be abolished and disbanded.

There are Constitutional issues here including the fact that the New York State Board of Elections is appointed by the Chairmen of the Democratic and Republican Parties. These are not elected officials. They are merely party pols. This is the reason there are always an even number of board members. The Democrats appoint two and the Republicans appoint two. In the New York City Board of Elections, there are 10 Commissioners, the Democratic County Chairmen appoint 5 and the Republican County Chairmen appoint 5.

However, nowadays there are only 8 sitting commissioners of the New York City Board of Elections. There are two vacant seats. The Bronx Democratic Party and the Manhattan Democratic Party Chairmen have not appointed replacements after those commissioners resigned. The three remaining Democratic Party Commissioners rarely speak at the meetings. This leaves the five Republican Party Commissioners basically to conduct the meetings.

It should be noted that the Bronx County Republican Party Chairman was arrested by the FBI last year on bribery charges. The New York Post reported that a $30,000 bribe was paid in order to secure the seat on the Board of Elections that the Bronx Republican Party Chairman had selected. "The fallen Bronx power broker said the deal was concocted after he reached out to Halloran in January 2013 for help ensuring that the City Council didn't replace one of Savino's hand-picked commissioners on the city's Board of Elections." See Ex-head of Bronx GOP admits taking bribe, but spreads blame, The New York Post November 12, 2013. He plead guilty and the City Councilman who arranged the deal was recently convicted and faces a long prison sentence. Yet, the Commissioner of Elections that he appointed is still serving on the Board of Elections.

So, a seat on the City Board of Elections is so valuable that a bribe will be paid to get on it. This should tell us that the duties of the board of elections is not merely "administrative".

Here in New York we presently have the same political system as they have in Iran. In Iran, Ayatollah Ali Khamenei decides who gets to run for election. Only those who have sufficient Islamic credentials as determined by the Ayatollah are allowed to run. The voters get to decide which of the candidates approved by the Ayatollah they will vote for. Nobody ever elected or voted for Ayatollah Ali Khamenei. He just rules the election process. Similarly, here in New York, the county party chairmen, one Republican and one Democrat, chose the Commissioners of Election and those Commissioners decide who gets to run for election.

Here is just one of many thousands of examples of corruption and favoritism in the Board of Elections. In 2013, one of the plaintiffs here, Sam Sloan, attempted to run for US Congress against Congressman Jose Serrano, the incumbent. Sloan filed line-by-line objections to the signatures submitted by Congressman Serrano, finding almost none of them valid. No doubt the reason Serrano did not have enough valid signatures was Serrano was out of favor with the Bronx Borough President Ruben Diaz, Jr. and thus the usual county party minions had not been sent out to collect Serrano's signatures.

When this matter came to a hearing before the New York City Board of Elections, Serrano was represented by Jerry Goldfeder, author of **Goldfeder's Modern Election Law.**

What happened can be seen on youtube.com at by searching for "4-24-14 Designating petition hearing for the June Federal Primary" which reaches the youtube video at https://www.youtube.com/watch?v=f3fSC2xtGNM or more easily by searching https://www.youtube.com/user/VoteTheNewWayNYC
When this case was called, both Jerry Goldfeder and Sam Sloan stood up. Then, Board of Elections General Counsel Steven H.

Richman objected to Sloan speaking even though Sloan was the aggrieved candidate and thus had the right to speak. Then Goldfeder stated that Sloan's objections had not been served on Serrano but had been served on Goldfeder instead and Serrano himself had been served one day late. Sloan replied that the objector had called Goldfeder pointing out that Serrano was in Washington DC on that day attending a Congressional hearing on Internet security and thus could not be personally served. To this, Goldfeder had replied to the objector to serve him instead at Goldfeder's residence on Central Park West.

At the hearing before the New York City Board of Elections, Goldfeder started to reply with the words, "I did have a conversation with him but I can say ... " He was addressing the statement that the Objector, Mr. Vega, had called him and asked about the address for service of process of the objections and that Mr. Goldfeder had given his own home address as the place for service. Just at the moment that Jerry H. Goldfeder was addressing that question, the President of the Board, Gregory C. Soumas, interrupted Goldfeder saying "Nothing has been said" and thus Mr. Goldfeder was not allowed to complete his sentence. All this can be heard at 6:01 on the youtube.com video. These hearings are now required by law to be posted on youtube.com and therefore it is proper to cite them.

It can be clearly seen on the youtube video that at just the moment Goldfeder was going to reply to the question of whether he had agreed to accept service of the line-by-line objections against his client Serrano, the President of the Board of Elections interrupted him and told him not to speak and ruled in his favor.

So, one of the best known election lawyers Jerry Goldfeder was interrupted from speaking so that he would not have to admit that he had agreed to accept service.

Had Serrano not been favored by the Commissioners, then Goldfeder would have had to admit that he had agreed to accept service and since Congressman Serrano had almost no valid signatures he would have been thrown off the ballot and Sloan would have been the sole Democratic Party candidate. Since the Democrats always win in the Bronx and the Republicans do not even bother to run candidates, Sloan would have been elected to US Congress. This is an example of how improper and illegal actions by the Board of Elections caused a candidate to be elected to US Congress who would not otherwise have been elected.

Neither the decision of the Albany federal court nor of the state courts made more than passing mention of the constitutional issues raised by the appellants. They just sloughed it off. Yet, there are obviously major constitutional issues with this entire system. It is obvious that under cases such as Avery v. Midland County 390 U.S. 474 (1968) and Board of Estimates vs. Morris, 489 US 688 (1988) the Board of Elections is an unconstitutional body.

The decision of the district court cited Queens County Republican Comm. ex rel. Maltese v. New York State Bd. Of Elections, 222 F. Supp. 2d 341, 349-51 (E.D.N.Y. 2002) (finding that sections 6-154 and 16-102 did not violate the plaintiffs' rights under the First Amendment) supports the views of the plaintiffs-appellants, not the views of the respondents. The district court below here stated: "The information before the Court shows that Defendants complied with the Election Law in invalidating the petitions at issue. See

N.Y. Elec. Law § 6-154." However, this "information" consists entirely of the Affirmation in Opposition filed by Kathleen O'Keefe, Democratic Party counsel to the State Board of Elections. Petitioner-Appellants dispute every statement made in her unverified affirmation. None of those statements are true, and petitioner-appellants are entitled to a fact-hearing on these issues.

The district court simply ignored the allegations of the complaint and made its decision without a fact hearing. Similarly there was no hearing in state court either except that Sam Sloan testified. The Board of Elections filed no papers in any of the courts and offered no testimony or evidence. Counsel for the Board of Elections did not call any witnesses nor contest the testimony of Sam Sloan. Thus, there is no contrary evidence in the record.

Plaintiff-Appellants are not complaining against Section 6-154. To the contrary, Plaintiff-Appellants are claiming the opposite, that the Board of Elections did not follow it. Plaintiff-Appellants want that rule followed strictly. The Board of Elections failure to follow Section 6-154 constitutes a violation of the Constitutional rights to Procedural Due Process. Goldberg v Kelly, 397 U.S. 254 (1970); Bell v Bunson, 402 U.S. 535 (1971); Sherbert v Verner, 374 U.S. 398 (1963)

Plaintiff-Appellants were thrown off the ballot without any notice, without any hearing, with no sufficiently specific objections having been filed, with no clerk's report, no referee, indeed nothing at all. The statements made by Kathleen O'Keefe in her affirmation come out of thin air. We do not know where her numbers come from. None of this was mentioned at the Board of Elections meeting on August 1, 2014. The discussion at that meeting lasted only 20 seconds and neither anybody on the board nor either of the counselors at the meeting gave any figures about the number of signatures or said anything about the age of the candidates. Also, the two letters opposing counsel put in the file when the case was before the Appellate Division were never seen by the Board of Elections and were generated after the meeting of the Board of Elections. They were not submitted nor marked into evidence when this case was before the Supreme Court. In short, all this should be sent back for a fact hearing before the District Court.

Here is what the relevant provision, Section 6-154, states:

> Nominations and designations; objections to
>
> 1. Any petition filed with the officer or board charged with the duty of receiving it shall be presumptively valid if it is in proper form and appears to bear the requisite number of signatures, authenticated in a manner prescribed by this chapter.
>
> 2. Written objections to any certificate of designation or nomination or to a nominating or designating petition or a petition for opportunity to ballot for public office or to a certificate of acceptance, a certificate of authorization, a certificate of declination or a certificate of substitution relating thereto may be filed by any voter registered to vote for such public office and to a designating petition or a petition for opportunity to ballot for party position or a certificate of substitution, a certificate of acceptance or a certificate of declination relating thereto by any voter enrolled to vote for such party position. Such objections shall be filed with the officer or board with whom the original petition or certificate is filed within three days after the filing of the petition or certificate to which objection is made, or within three days after the last day to file such a certificate, if no such certificate is filed except that if any person nominated by an

> independent nominating petition, is nominated as a party candidate for the same office by a party certificate filed, or a party nomination made after the filing of such petition, the written objection to such petition may be filed within three days after the filing of such party certificate or the making of such party nomination. When such an objection is filed, specifications of the grounds of the objections shall be filed within six days thereafter with the same officer or board and if specifications are not timely filed, the objection shall be null and void. Each such officer or board is hereby empowered to make rules in reference to the filing and disposition of such petition, certificate, objections and specifications.
>
> 3. When a determination is made that a certificate or petition is insufficient, such officer or board shall give notice of the determination forthwith by mail to each candidate named in the petition or certificate, and, if the determination is made upon specified objections, the objector shall be notified.

In fact none of this was done. The petitions were filed nominating these candidates on July 8, 2014. These petitions were marked "Valid" by the Board of Elections at that time. See http://www.elections.ny.gov:8080/reports/rwservlet?cmdkey=whofiled The Board of Elections website shows the four volumes were filed totaling 4065 pages. They remained marked valid for nearly one month until August 4, 2014 when, without notice or the opportunity for a hearing, they were changed from "valid" to "invalid".

These candidates were never notified that such a change was imminent. The objectors were also not notified, no doubt because the "specific objections" were in summary form and were not line-by-line objections and not up the standard required by the Board of Elections.

The following cross examination took place on pages 27-28 the transcript which is on pages A-126-127 Appendix on Appeal:

(Sam Sloan - Cross by Ms. O'Keefe)

Q Mr. Sloan, are you aware of how many sheets of paper are in a ream of paper? Are you aware of how many are in a ream? You buy paper, copy paper in reams?
A I suppose there is 500. I don't know.
Q That's right. And four thousand pages would be how many reams?
A I guess simple multiplication. It would be eight.
Q It would be eight. Does that stack of pages look like it's eight reams of paper?
A I'm not an expert on paper size.

Here is what Democratic Party Counsel to the Board of Elections, Kathleen O'Keefe, said to the court (See Transcript):

> "With respect to that particular candidate, the Board received time specific and general objections from two different objectors. And when the Board met on August 1st the Board voted in public, and they are on a video that's available on YouTube, because they do have their meetings in public, with respect to that candidate, that she did not meet both the signature requirements, as well as the age requirement, and they held her Petition invalid."

However, none of this is true. It is urgently requested that this court play the youtube video of that meeting. It will be seen that this is not at all what really happened. The agenda for that meeting is at http://www.elections.ny.gov/NYSBOE/news/MeetingMinutes/Agenda08012014.pdf

A link to the video of that meeting is at the top of http://www.elections.ny.gov/2014Meetings.html

Opposing counsel claims that the above statements can be found on youtube. However, none of these statements are on youtube. One needs to play the youtube.com video of the meeting on the New York State Board of Elections on August 1, 2014.

The important part of the video regarding Sam Sloan, Nanad Bach,

Geeta Rankoth and Neil Grimaldi starts at 6:20 and goes on only about 20 seconds. There, an attorney for the Republican Party, Kimberly Galvin, says she has an addendum to the motion to the board by having Sam Sloan, Nanad Bach, Geeta Rakoth and Neil Grimaldi removed from the ballot. No member of the board mentions those names. Nothing is said by any member of the Board about Geeta Rankoth or anybody else not having enough signatures or about their age. No mention is made by anybody about the age requirement to run for Comptroller.

Geeta Rankoth, a college student and a graduate of Bronx High School of Science, herself had written to the Board stating the following: "I wish to add that it is a violation of federal law to discriminate against me because of my age. Specifically it violates the Age Discrimination in Employment Act of 1967 and other state and federal laws." Neither the Board of Elections nor the Supreme Court nor the Appellate Division were informed of this letter or this issue.

By doing a search on youtube.com for "NYSBOE - 08.01.2014" one can find the actual video of the meeting. Ms. Kathleen O'Keefe is shown on the video. She was there although she said nothing. Next to her is a man with white hair, Robert A. Brehm, Co-Executive Director of the Board of Elections. What the video shows is Commissioner Kellner moves to start the agenda with section 4a and then reads off from a sheet of paper a list of 14 candidates and slates who are bring thrown off because of objections. After he finishes reading the list, the Republican Party attorney Kimberly Galvin interrupts by saying that she has an addendum of four names of people she wants thrown off the ballot. She attempts to hand up a sheet with the names but is told to read it instead. Those names are Sam Sloan, Nanad Bach,

Geeta Rankoth and Neil Grimaldi.

Commissioner Kellner then goes on to read a list of names of candidates who failed to file acceptances and are being thrown off for that reason.

After concluding these lists, Commissioner Kellner states, "We need to make a motion to adopt the Prima Facia list as reported in writing and as I just read."

This is followed by "So Moved" and "Passed".

However, the names of Sam Sloan, Nanad Bach, Geeta Rankoth and Neil Grimaldi were not on the lists "just read" by Commissioner Kellner. Those four names were only mentioned orally by Kimberly Galvin, who is not a member of the board. Neither Commissioner Kellner nor any of the other Commissioners mentioned those names. Therefore, Sam Sloan, Nanad Bach, Geeta Rankoth and Neil Grimaldi were not legally thrown off the ballot.

The Court below cited **Fischer v. Suffolk County Bd. of Elections**, **No. 08-CV-4171, 2009 WL 2524859 (E.D.N.Y. Aug. 14, 2009)**. However, that case was only concerned with the counting of the signatures. Moreover, that decision supports the position of Plaintiffs-Appellants. Appellants contend that the Board of Elections had no jurisdiction to count the signatures. They can only count the signatures if somebody objected.

If the Board of Elections is allowed to count the signatures any time it feels like, the result will be that it will target those candidates whom it dislikes and count their signatures. Since the Board is appointed by the party leaders, they will target those persons whom they would prefer not to be on the ballot. This is unconstitutional.

The way this system was set up the Board of Elections is not supposed to do any counting at all. The objectors are supposed to do the counting. Then they are supposed to submit a Line-by-line Specific Objection telling exactly what is wrong with the petitions. None of the objectors to Rankoth or Grimaldi submitted line-by-line objections. They just submitted vague generalized objections. That is the reason why when the Commissioner Kellner read a list of objections at the meeting on August 1, 2014, he did not include in his list the objectors to Rankoth or Grimaldi.

Fischer v. Suffolk County Bd. of Elections, shows exactly what is supposed to happened but did not happen in the instant case. There was a hearing before the Board of Elections. This was followed by a validating proceeding. During that proceeding the court restored 42 signatures that had been thrown off by the board. However, that was not enough to get Fischer back on the ballot. A district court case was filed that resulted in three reported decisions.

There the court stated: "Plaintiff has made is clear that he is not arguing the constitutionality of the election laws, nor does he argue that he was denied an independent constitutional right."

However, here Plaintiff-Appellants contend both that the Board of Elections is unconstitutional and that the plaintiff-appellants were denied a variety of constitutional rights.

The Board of Elections is unconstitutional because they are appointed by the Chairmen of the Republican and Democratic Parties. These chairmen want to control the election process so as to insure that only the candidates they favor have a realistic chance to get elected. One cannot even remember a case in the last several decades when anybody not nominated by either the Republican or the Democratic Party leadership was elected to statewide office. The members of the minor but recognized parties, the Green, Conservative, Working Families and Independence parties, can nominate candidates but they have never been elected. More importantly, the much larger group voters who are not enrolled in any party are left out in the cold.

Within the parties, in the New York City Board of Elections each borough gets two commissioners, one Republican and one Democratic. However, Kings County (Brooklyn) has a population of 2.5 million whereas Richmond County (Staten Island) has a population of 470,000. Thus, one vote in Richmond County has the same power as five votes in Brooklyn.

The state court judges are also appointed politically. In order to became a state court judge one must be nominated by either the Republican or the Democratic Party. If a judge makes decisions the party chairman does not like, he will simply not be renominated and will lose his job, as happened in the Lopez-Torres Case. N.Y. State Board of Elections v. Lopez Torres, 552 U.S. 196 (2008) One cannot expect the New York State Court judges to put themselves out of work by declaring the system by which they got elected to be unconstitutional.

We understand that the district court judge here was in a hurry to make a decision in time for the election and we appreciate that errors were inevitable. However, she simply adopted all of the "facts" as set forth by opposing counsel and ignored the allegations of the complaint. The district court decision needs to be reviewed and reversed. We do not know where these numbers of signatures came from. The Supreme Court judge said that the last page of the petitions was page number 1402. However, that was only the last page of volume four. There were three other volumes and a total of 4065 pages. Perhaps the staff of the Board of Elections only counted volume four and did not count the other three volumes. This may explain why it is said that there are only 4,000-5,000 signatures, whereas there are actually 4,000 sheets of petition signatures. Again, there is no clerk's report or other documentation to support these statements.

The counselor for the plaintiffs-appellants here is active in election law cases. He represented clients in six different election cases in Bronx Supreme Court this August. On the day when the Board of Elections was meeting in Albany on August 1, 2014, he was appearing in four other contested election cases in Bronx Supreme Court where he was representing clients. One of these was the Quinones case which resulted in another case in district court. **Moore and Quinones vs. New York City Board of Elections**, **14-CV-6643 (SDNY)**. For this reason he could not make it to Albany for the meeting plus there was no notice that these four candidates (including himself) would be at issue during this meeting, as they were not on the agenda. He has stated that in his years of experience in election cases, he has never seen a case like this one where there were no objections, no clerk's report, no hearing, no vote to throw them off, no due process of any kind.

One of the candidates here has the distinction of having argued orally before the United States Supreme Court an analogous case. In **S.E.C. vs Samuel H. Sloan**, **436 US 103 (1978)** he argued successfully that the United States Securities and Exchange

Commission had been violating their own laws and regulations since 1934 by suspending trading in securities for more than ten days without notice or a hearing. By wining that 9-0 decision, he brought to an end the practice of the SEC of suspending trading in securities for long periods of time.

Here, he states that the New York State Board of Elections violated its own rules, including especially Section 6-154, by removing candidates from the ballot without objections, without notice, without a hearing, without anything at all.

Queens County Republican Comm. ex rel. Maltese v. New York State Bd. of Elections, 222 F. Supp. 2d 341, 349-51 (E.D.N.Y. 2002), cited by the court, supports this view. There the court stated that the fact that any voter of any party can object to a petition provides adequate safeguards to voter fraud. We agree with and support that decision. What the Board of Elections here is stating is that it can throw any candidate it likes off the ballot without any objections by anybody. That is clearly unconstitutional.

ARGUMENT

The plaintiff-appellants are candidates for office or else are voters who support these candidates, who signed their petitions and who want to vote for them for election. The candidates were on the ballot since July 8, 2014 but were thrown off the ballot by the New York State Board of Elections on August 1, 2014.

Objections were filed to the candidacy of Geeta Rankoth for Comptroller. One objection was that Geeta Rankoth was not an enrolled member of the Democratic Party. However, this was mistaken, as Geeta Rankoth was in fact an enrolled member of the

Democratic Party.

No objections were filed against candidate Sam Sloan for Governor. Nevertheless, the Board of Elections, arbitrarily and capriciously and without any warning, notice nor any hearing threw Sloan, Bach, Grimaldi and Rankoth off the ballot in violation of the Rules of the Board of Elections including especially Section 6-154 of New York Election Law. The Board of Elections simply had no jurisdiction to remove these candidates from the ballot.

Statements made by opposing counsel about what the Board of Elections found or the number of petition signatures submitted by the candidates are pure fabrications by opposing counsel, as the Board of Elections made no such findings nor had any hearing or factual determination. These statements are pure inventions by opposing counsel.

Plaintiffs-Appellants contend that the entire Board of Elections is unconstitutional for several reasons. The Commissioners of Election are not elected officials nor are they appointed by elected officials. They are appointed by the Republican and Democratic Party Chairmen and those chairmen are not elected either. The commissioners are simply political insiders, cronies and hacks. The other recognized parties including the Green, Conservative, Working Families and Independence Parties get no representation on the Board of Elections nor do the millions of voters who are not enrolled members of any party get any representation or say-so on the Board of Elections. The whole set-up is so obviously unconstitutional that nobody can defend it. The Board of Elections has been doing this for years since the days of Boss Tweed and getting away with it. They should be going to jail, like Tweed did.

Because the Board of Elections engaged in massive fraud in throwing these and many other qualified candidates off the ballot (including other candidates represented by plaintiff's counsel such as Quinones) the entire election should be declared invalid and thrown out and redone with all the candidates restored.

Plaintiff-appellants contend that this case should be remanded for a fact hearing. Plaintiffs will show that for years the Board of Elections has been abusing its authority by throwing perfectly qualified candidates off the ballot. Because the Commissioners of Elections are appointed by the Democratic and Republican Party State and County Chairmen, who are not elected officials, these chairmen have a vested interest in protecting their favored candidates and preventing any insurgents from within the party such as the candidates here or from outside from getting on the ballot.

Plaintiffs contend that under many court decisions including The Board of Estimates vs. Morris, 489 US 688 (1988) the entire set-up is unconstitutional.

The standard is "one man one vote" and is the established law of the nation, Gray v. Sanders, 372 U.S. 368 (1963), Reynolds v Sims, 377 U.S. 533 (1964); Baker v. Carr, 369 U.S. 186 (1962); Gaffney v. Cummings, 412 U.S. 735 (1973); Seaman v. Fedourich, 16 NY 2d 94; Moore v. Ogilvie, 394 U.S. 814 (1969)

POINT ONE

The Judge's decision failed to differentiate between between an educational administrative body and the New York Board of

Elections, which is an executive body with quasi-judicial functions and decides issues involving the United States Constitutional Rights of Voters to their choice of candidates and the candidate's United States rights.

The Board of Estimates vs. Morris, 489 US 688 (1988) governs this case rather than the much earlier decision of Sailors et al vs. Board of Education of Kent et al, 387 US 105 (1967) because the New York State Board of Elections is much more similar to the Board of Estimates of the City of New York and the Board of Estimates case is later. The case of Sailors, supra concerned only the election of county school board members whose electors are elected by the people, where a school board member has a non-legislative office for which no election is involved or required. The Sailors case required "a subordinate governmental instrumentality created by the state to assist in carrying out of state governmental functions".

The court in Sailors based their decision on the fact that the work done by the Kent County was basically minor.

The Board of Elections of New York has a quasi-judicial functions invalidating candidates from the ballot and this involve decisions regarding United States Constitutional rights of voters and candidate. Therefore the standard of "one man one vote" is the established law of the nation, Gray v. Sanders, 372 U.S. 368 (1963), Reynolds v Sims, 377 U.S. 533 (1964); Baker v. Carr, 369 U.S. 186 (1962); Gaffney v. Cummings, 412 U.S. 735 (1973); Seaman v. Fedourich, 16 NY 2d 94; Moore v. Ogilvie, 394 U.S. 814 (1969), Oliver v. Bd of Education, 306 F Supp 1286.

Restraints imposed by the constitution on the states can never be circumvented by local bodies to whom the state delegates authority like The Board of Elections for the State of New York and the Board of Elections for The City of New York. Standard Computing Scale Company v Farrell, 249 U.S. 571 (1919); Cooper v Aaron, 358 U.S. 1 (1958).

The other case the judge cited is Cohanim vs. New York City Board of Education, 204 F. Supp. 2d 452, 453 (2002) involved only how New York City Board of Education members are selected. Their Education Board is in no way comparable to the New York State Board of Elections which has quasi-judicial and executive functions regarding the United States Constitutional Rights of voters in having candidates of their choice and the United States Constitutional Rights of candidates.

In Hedley vs. Junior College District, 397 US 50 (1970), the United States Supreme Court dispensed with the standard set forth in Sailors, supra and held that the election to a position that performed a governmental function as the New York States Board of Elections does must accord with "one man one vote"

The Fourteenth Amendment section 1 states "nor deny any person within its jurisdiction the equal protection of the law". All voters including members of all other parties other than Republican or Democratic have no voice or representation on the Board of Elections and deprives them of equal protection of the laws. Board of Estimate of City of New York v. Morris 489 U.S. 688 (1989).

The equal protection clause forbids the elevation of a small class of super-voters granted an extraordinary powerful franchise as does the Board of Elections for Republican and Democratic only voters. Brown v. Thomson, 462 U.S. 835 (1983).

The Board of Elections in not representing smaller parties violates minority rights of smaller parties set forth in Section 2 of The Federal Voting Rights Act 42 U.S. 1973 et seq,

The New York State Board of Elections and their local boards must be held unconstitutional because they fail to represent millions of voters and they violate "one man one vote". Dunn v. Blumstein, 405 U.S. 330 (1972); Abate v. Mundt, 403 U.S. 182 (1971).

The fact the Board makes quasi-judicial decisions and is made up of members who have an interest in the outcome makes them an unfair judicial body thus violating procedural due process of the Fourteenth Amendment. The Board members chosen by the chairmen of the Republican and Democratic parties is especially prejudicial when they vote on issues of ballot access by opponents of the individuals who appointed them as was done to this slate of candidates including Sam Sloan for Governor.

The Board of Elections has not heretofore produce one valid and sustainable legal precedent for the continuation of The Board of Elections in the face of all the existing cases cited herein that prove and illustrate clearly that The Board violates The Equal Protection Clause and "one man one vote" legal precedents that protect individuals like the petition signers and all the candidates that are on this slate as Petitioners. Reynolds v Sims, 377 U.S. 533 (1964), Connor v. Finch, 431 U.S. 407, 420 (1977); Cohen v Mahoney, 410 F. Supp 1286;

Grisbaum v. McKeithen, 339 F. Supp. 267 (1971), Latino Political Action Commitee, Inc. vs. City of Boston, 784 F.2d 409 (1986); Iannucci v. Bd. of Supervisors of Washington County, 20 N.Y. 2D 244,249, Franklin v Mandeville ,26 N.Y. 2D 65, 69-70; Franklin v Krause 32 N.Y. 2D 234; Wesberry v. Sanders, 376 U.S. 1 (1964); Curcio v Boyle 147 A.D. 194; Jackson v Nassau County Bd. of Supervisors, 818 F. Supp. 98; Avery v. Midland County, 390 U.S. 474 (1968), Whitcomb v. Chavis, 403 U.S. 124, 145-146 (1976), Karcher v Daggett, 46 U.S. 725,741 (1971).

POINT TWO

The Court had insufficient evidence as a matter of law to invalidate these candidates from being on the ballot and violating the United States constitutional rights of their petition signers. The Board of Elections violated procedural due process in invalidating the petitions without notice to the Plaintiffs - Candidates and not having a viable hearing at The Board as required by The Fourteenth Amendment and the due process clause. Goldberg v Kelly, 397 U.S. 254 (1970); Bell v Bunson, 402 U.S. 535 (1971); Sherbert v Verner, 374 U.S. 398 (1963)

This case involves the rights of five voters, unlike the case in New York Supreme Court. These five voters were not part of the state board's case and they have separate constitutional rights to have the candidates of their choice on the ballot and the prior case cannot preclude their rights. See Reynolds v Sims,

377 U.S. 533 (1964); <u>Baker v. Carr</u>, 369 U.S. 186 (1962).

This case is different than the cases cited by Miss O'Keefe because in this case the basic constitutional rights of Sam Sloan and Nenad Bach were violated in that there were no objections of specifications filed against them. They did not receive their rights under the 14th amendment to notice and a hearing before their United States Constitutional rights to run for election were removed from them.

Opposing Counsel failed to mention that there was never any evidence of specifications or objections filed against Sam Sloan or Nenad Bach. The specifications and arguments about insufficient age filed against Geeta Rankoth are not objections to the candidacy of Sam Sloan and Nenad Bach as there were no objections filed against them as to the insufficiency of their age or candidacy.

The case mentioned of <u>Fischer v. Suffolk County Bd. of Elections</u>, No. 08-cv-4171, 2009 WL 2524859 (E.D.N.Y. Aug. 14, 2009) does not apply to this case because in that case there was no claim of constitutional rights violated. That case only had to do with the inadequate amount of signatures.

The cover sheets claimed that the candidates had a sufficient amount of signatures and thus there was no basis to invalidate them without a hearing. The New York State Supreme Court and Appellate Division statement of the jurisdictional failure by not naming the objectors does not apply to this court because there is no such rule in this court and because of this the state court did not deal with the constitutional issues.

The US Constitution protects under the 14th Amendment these petition signers and they should not be allowed to have their rights considered in this case whereas they were not in the proceeding before the Board of Elections.

The State Board of Elections and the New York City Board of Elections are not just administrative bodies. They have executive and judicial functions which violate candidate's rights. These boards are selected by Chairmen of the Republican and Democratic parties and are prejudicial because of their judicial functions in throwing candidates off the ballot after a hearing, thus violating their due process rights to fair hearing before a fair trier of the facts. **Avery v. Midland County**, 390 U.S. 474 (1968).

In **Board of Estimate of City of New York v. Morris**, 489 U.S. 688 (1988) decided March 22, 1989, the United States Supreme Court held the Board of Estimates was illegally constituted because it violated the Equal Protection Clause of the 14th Amendment to the constitution. So, the New York Board of Estimates was found to be null and void as a government agency, citing **Reynolds v Sims**, 377 U.S. 533 (1964) and **Abate v. Mundt**, 403 U.S. 182 (1971). The Board of Elections completely denies voter equality by ignoring the voting rights of all voters not Republican or Democrat. Also, Republican Voters have more voting power than Democrats because Democrats far exceed Republican voters in numbers. The NY Board of Elections and the New York City Board of Elections violate the Equal Protection Clause based on the disparity between Republicans and Democrats and the fact that so many millions of voters have no representative on the Board of Elections. This inequitable system at the board places the most prejudicial people as executives or board members by how they are chosen by representatives of the Democratic Party Chairperson and Republican Party Chairperson. Therefore, they cannot constitute a just body or forum to make legal and binding decisions.

This year at a recent July 2014 hearing of the New York City Board of Elections, Eliot Quinones was placed on the ballot by the clerk's report. Then without notice a new Board of Elections clerk's report put him off the ballot. These decisions excluded voters who properly signed the petition. New York Board of Elections clerk's report fundamentally put him off the ballot based on improper decisions excluding voters who properly signed the petition. The New York City Board of Elections allows one representative for Richmond and one representative for Brooklyn despite the fact that Brooklyn has five times as many voters as Richmond. This is exactly the reason why the Board of Estimates was found illegal by the United States Supreme Court. The Board of Elections in the City of New York is part of the New York State Board of Elections.

Reynolds v Sims, 377 U.S. 533 (1964) established that the Fourteenth Amendment of the United States Constitution established the principle of the equal protection clause and equal protection of the law. Required the Alabama legislature voting to be based on population. The Board of Elections ignores this landmark case and principle. This case stands for the fundamental principle of legislative government in the United States of equal representation for equal numbers of people. The right to vote is a personal right. The idea that one group can be granted greater voting strength as the board does excluding all Democratic and Republican voters than another is inconsistent with standards for popular representative government. Under the equal protection clause a claim of debasement of the right to vote through mal apportionment represents a practicable controversy and the equal protection clause provides manageable standards for the lower courts to determine the constitutionality of a state legislative appointment scheme, citing Baker v. Carr, 369 U.S. 186 (1962). In addition it undercuts states voters rights and the duly established United States Constitutional rights.

Oliver vs. Board of Education, 306 F. Supp. 1286, No. 69 Civ 2130, United States District Court for the Southern District of New York held that a statute creating the New York City School Board was unconstitutional where the statute provided that citizens of each borough elected one member of the school board. Statute diluted votes of the most populous boroughs. The way the New York State Board of Elections and New York City Board of Elections is organized violates the rights of all voters not Republican or Democratic and gives each Republican voter more power than each Democrat which is unequal and illegal. Also, voting procedures including proxy voting must follow one man one vote Atkins v. Monahan, 91 Misc. 2d 499, 399 NYS 2d 166.

Sergey v. King's County Republican Party, 459 F.2d 308 invalidated a county political party's rule on the voting procedure of the one party where each county committee member has an equal vote weighed according to the number of Republican voters in the district he represents. This violates the one-man one-vote principle established by the Supreme Court as a voters constitutional right. The amount of Democratic Party voters far exceeds the amount of Republican Party voters and gives one Republican and Democratic members equal power and not representing all other voters and Republican or Democratic violated the one-man one-vote constitutional law principle. The equal protection clause applies one man one vote even to count committeemen. Not giving a group the right to representation violates their constitutional rights and discriminates against them. See Moore v. Ogilvie, 394 U.S. 814 (1969)

Fisher vs. Board of Supervisors, 59 Misc. 953; 301 NYS 2d 310 citing Seaman v. Fedourich, 16 NY 2d 94, 101 required the "one man one vote" principle required each votes be given equal weight. The Board of Elections excludes the rights of millions of voters and unfairly gives Republican voters more importance than an equal number of Democratic voters. See Burton vs. Schmidt, 128 Misc. 270.

The basic exclusion of the Board of Elections of the rights of millions of voters not Republican and Democrat is unequitably a violation of the equal protection clause of the Fourteenth Amendment see Reynolds v Sims, 377 U.S. 533 (1964), Board of Estimate of City of New York v. Morris, 489 U.S. 688 (1989).

The New York City Board of Elections has a long history of violating the United States voter's rights and insurgent Democratic and Republican voters rights including none of the other parties by the illegal manner that members of the Board of Elections in New York City as elsewhere are chosen by the New York City Republican and Democratic Party political readers. This violates the Fourteenth Amendment due process requirements because the forum is not a just body and it is constituted in a way by giving undue and improper power to representatives of the Democratic and Republican Chairmen and their representatives who claim to be made a quasi-judicial body making legally binding decisions which they have harmful by their extensive officer and bureau members are selected illegally by the Political Democratic Party Chairmen and Republican Chairmen. It would be proper and legal only to have a civil service Board of Elections. The members of the Board of Elections or an independent non-partisan non-prejudicial system of choosing Board of Election members statewide and in New York City and in each of our great New York County. The Respondents have refused to provide a legal basis in opposition because there is none.

Whereas Petitioner is requesting an opportunity to subpoena witnesses and present evidence about the long history of political corruption caused by the illegal and improper manner the New York State Board of Elections and New York City Board of Elections are illegally formed, violative of the equal protection clause one man one vote and basic justice

Conclusion

The New York State Board of Elections must be found in violation of the United States Constitution and thus abolished as presently constituted.

CERTIFICATE OF COMPLIANCE

This brief complies with the type-volume limitation of Fed. R. App. P. 28.1(e)(2)(a) because this brief contains 8,407 words, excluding the parts of the brief exempted by Fed. R. App. P. 32(a)(7)(B)(iii).

This brief complies with the typeface requirements of Fed. R. App. P. 32(a)(5) and the type style requirements of Fed. R. App. P. 32(a)(6) because this brief has been prepared Courier New 12 point Bold.

Dated: Bronx, New York November 21, 2014

Neil V. Grimaldi
Counsel for Plaintiffs
2860 Buhre Avenue, Suite 1E
Bronx, New York 10461
646-229-7974

14-3342

United States Court of Appeals

for the

Second Circuit

Sam Sloan, Neil V. Grimaldi, Nereida Narveaz, Veniada Quinones, Millie Quinones, Tiara Lawrence, Trina Jackson,

Plaintiffs - Appellants

v.

New York State Board of Elections, 40 North Pearl Street, Suite 5 Albany, NY 12207, Eric T. Schneiderman, as Attorney General of the State of New York, Douglas A. Kellner, as Commissioner of the New York State Board of Elections, Andrew Spano, as Commissioner of the New York State Board of Elections, James A. Walsh, as Commissioner of the New York State Board of Elections, Gregory P. Peterson, as Commissioner of the New York State Board of Elections,

Defendants - Appellees.

ON APPEAL from the UNITED STATES DISTRICT COURT
for the NORTHERN DISTRICT OF NEW YORK

District Court Case No. 1:14-cv-01071 (MAD/CFH)

APPENDIX ON APPEAL

Neil V. Grimaldi
Counsel for Plaintiffs-Appellants
2860 Buhre Avenue, Suite 1E
Bronx, New York 10461
646-229-7974

Appendix on Appeal

Table of Contents

APPEAL

U.S. District Court
Northern District of New York – Main Office (Syracuse) [LIVE – Version 6.1] (Albany)
CIVIL DOCKET FOR CASE #: 1:14–cv–01071–MAD–CFH

Sloan et al v. New York State Board Of Elections et al
Assigned to: U.S. District Judge Mae A. D'Agostino
Referred to: Magistrate Judge Christian F. Hummel
Case in other court: Supreme Court of NYS Appellate Division– Third Dpt, 03–00014
Cause: 28:1331 Fed. Question

Date Filed: 08/29/2014
Jury Demand: None
Nature of Suit: 441 Civil Rights: Voting
Jurisdiction: Federal Question

Plaintiff

Sam Sloan represented by **Sam Sloan**
2860 Buhre Avenue
Suite 1E
New York, NY 10461
PRO SE

Plaintiff

Neil V. Grimaldi represented by **Neil V. Grimaldi**
2860 Buhre Ave.
Suite 1E
New York, NY 10461
646 229–7974
PRO SE

Plaintiff

Nereida Narveaz represented by **Nereida Narveaz**
1815 Davidson
Bronx, NY 10453
PRO SE

Plaintiff

Veniada Quinones represented by **Veniada Quinones**
1815 Davidson
Bronx, NY 10453
PRO SE

Plaintiff

Millie Quinones represented by **Millie Quinones**
1921 Jerome Avenue
Bronx, NY 10453
PRO SE

Plaintiff

Tiara Lawrence represented by **Tiara Lawrence**
1921 Jerome Avenue
Bronx, NY 10453
PRO SE

Plaintiff

Trina Jackson represented by **Trina Jackson**
1921 Jerome Avenue
Bronx, NY 10453
PRO SE

V.

Defendant

New York State Board Of Elections 40 North Pearl Street, Suite 5 Albany, NY 12207	represented by	**Kathleen O'Keefe** New York State Board of Elections Office of Special Counsel 40 North Pearl Street, Suite 5 Albany, NY 12207–2729 518–474–2063 Fax: 518–486–6627 Email: kathleen.okeefe@elections.ny.gov *LEAD ATTORNEY* *ATTORNEY TO BE NOTICED*

Defendant

Eric T. Schneiderman *as Attorney General of the State of New York*	represented by	**David Fruchter** Office of Attorney General – Albany State of New York The Capitol Albany, NY 12224 518–473–5095 Fax: 518–473–1572 Email: david.fruchter@ag.ny.gov *LEAD ATTORNEY* *ATTORNEY TO BE NOTICED*

Defendant

Douglas A. Kellner *as Commissioner of the New York State Board of Elections*	represented by	**Kathleen O'Keefe** (See above for address) *LEAD ATTORNEY* *ATTORNEY TO BE NOTICED*

Defendant

Andrew Spano *as Commissioner of the New York State Board of Elections*	represented by	**Kathleen O'Keefe** (See above for address) *LEAD ATTORNEY* *ATTORNEY TO BE NOTICED*

Defendant

James A. Walsh *as Commissioner of the New York State Board of Elections*	represented by	**Kathleen O'Keefe** (See above for address) *LEAD ATTORNEY* *ATTORNEY TO BE NOTICED*

Defendant

Gregory P. Peterson *as Commissioner of the New York State Board of Elections*	represented by	**Kathleen O'Keefe** (See above for address) *LEAD ATTORNEY* *ATTORNEY TO BE NOTICED*

Date Filed	#	Docket Text
08/29/2014	1	COMPLAINT against New York State Board Of Elections, Eric T. Schneiderman (Filing fee $400 receipt number ALB008721) filed by Sam Sloan, Neil V. Grimaldi. (Attachments: # 1 Civil Cover Sheet)(tab) (Entered: 08/29/2014)
08/29/2014	2	G.O. 25 FILING ORDER ISSUED: Initial Conference set for 11/25/2014 09:00 AM in Albany before Magistrate Judge Christian F. Hummel. Civil Case Management Plan must be filed and Mandatory Disclosures are to be exchanged by the parties on or before 11/18/2014. (Pursuant to Local Rule 26.2, mandatory disclosures are to be

		exchanged among the parties but are NOT to be filed with the Court.) (tab) (Entered: 08/29/2014)
08/29/2014	3	Summons Issued as to New York State Board Of Elections, Eric T. Schneiderman. (tab) (Entered: 08/29/2014)
08/29/2014	4	MOTION for Order to Show Cause/Preliminary Injunction by Neil V. Grimaldi, Sam Sloan. (Attachments: # 1 Exhibit(s), # 2 Exhibit(s), # 3 Exhibit(s), # 4 Exhibit(s), # 5 Exhibit(s))(tab) (Entered: 08/29/2014)
09/02/2014	5	NOTICE/VERIFICATION by Trina Jackson, Tiara Lawrence, Nereida Narveaz, Millie Quinones, Veniada Quinones re 1 Complaint as named plaintiffs in this action. (tab) (Entered: 09/02/2014)
09/02/2014	6	ORDER TO SHOW CAUSE re 4 MOTION for Preliminary Injunction filed by Sam Sloan, Neil V. Grimaldi: The Court hereby ORDERS that Defendants show cause, if there be any, to this Court by submission on papers as ordered herein, before the Honorable Mae A. D'Agostino, United States District CourtJudge at the United States Courthouse, 445 Broadway, Albany, New York, why an order should not be made and entered herein restoring Sam Sloan on the ballot as a candidate for Governor of New York State, Nenad Bach as a candidate for Lieutenant Governor of New York State, Geeta Rankoth as a candidate for Comptroller of New York State, and Neil V. Grimaldi as a candidatefor Attorney General of New York State, in the Democratic Primary to be held on September 9, 2014; and the Court further ORDERS that Plaintiffs shall serve a copy of this Order to Show Cause together with a copy of the papers upon which it is based, by delivery to the New York State Board of Electionsat 40 N. Pearl Street, Albany, New York 12207 and upon the Attorney General of the State of New York at the Robert Abrams Building, Albany, New York, on or before 1:00 p.m. on September 3, 2014 and upon the other Defendants by certified mail; and the Court further ORDERS that Defendants shall serve and file any opposition to Plaintiffs' motion on or before September 5, 2014 at 1:00 p.m.; and the Court further ORDERS that Plaintiffs shall serve and file any reply papers on or before September 5, 2014 at 5:00 p.m.; and the Court further ORDERS that no personal appearance is required the papers will be taken on submission unless otherwise directed by the Court. Signed by U.S. District Judge Mae A. D'Agostino on 9/2/14. [plaintiff's mailed copies on 9/2/14 and informed over the phone on 9/2/14](ban) (Entered: 09/02/2014)
09/05/2014	7	RESPONSE TO ORDER TO SHOW CAUSE filed by Eric T. Schneiderman. (Attachments: # 1 Declaration Declaration of Service)(Fruchter, David) (Entered: 09/05/2014)
09/05/2014	8	RESPONSE in Opposition re 4 MOTION for Preliminary Injunction filed by New York State Board Of Elections. (Attachments: # 1 Memorandum of Law, # 2 Exhibit(s), # 3 Exhibit(s), # 4 Exhibit(s))(O'Keefe, Kathleen) (Entered: 09/05/2014)
09/05/2014	9	REPLY to Response to Motion re 4 MOTION for Preliminary Injunction filed by Neil V. Grimaldi. (ban) Modified on 9/8/2014 (ban) – Reply emailed to Judge D'Agostino's CRD at 4:56pm on 9/5/14. (Entered: 09/08/2014)
09/08/2014	10	MEMORANDUM–DECISION AND ORDER denying 4 Motion for Preliminary Injunction: The Court hereby ORDERS that Plaintiffs' motion for injunctive relief is DENIED; and the Court further ORDERS that the Clerk of the Court shall serve a copy of this Memorandum–Decision and Order on the parties in accordance with the Local Rules. Signed by U.S. District Judge Mae A. D'Agostino on 9/8/14. [all non ecf parties mailed a copy 9/8/14] (ban) (Entered: 09/08/2014)
09/09/2014	11	NOTICE OF INTERLOCUTORY APPEAL as to 10 Order on Motion for Preliminary Injunction, by Neil V. Grimaldi, Trina Jackson, Tiara Lawrence, Nereida Narveaz, Millie Quinones, Veniada Quinones, Sam Sloan. Filing fee $ 505, receipt number ALB008739. (tab) (Entered: 09/09/2014)
09/09/2014	12	ELECTRONIC NOTICE AND CERTIFICATION sent to US Court of Appeals re 11 Notice of Interlocutory Appeal. (tab) (Entered: 09/09/2014)
09/12/2014	13	Mail Returned as Undeliverable regarding the # 6 Order sent to Veniada Quinones at the Address of 1815 Davidson, Bronx, NY 10453. Envelope marked as "Return to Sender – Attempted–Not Known – Unable to Forward." (mc) (Entered: 09/12/2014)

U.S. DISTRICT COURT
N.D. OF N.Y.
FILED

AUG 29 2014

LAWRENCE K. BAERMAN, CLERK
ALBANY

UNITED STATES DISTRICT COURT
NORTHERN DISTRICT OF NEW YORK

Sam Sloan, Nenad Bach, Geeta Rankoth, Neil V. Grimaldi, Millie Quinones, Trina Jackson, Tiara Lawrence, Nereida Narveaz and Veniada Quinones,

Plaintiffs

COMPLAINT 1:14-CV-1071 MAD/CFH

-against-

Douglas A. Kellner, Andrew Spano, James A. Walsh, Gregory P. Peterson, Commissioners and Constituting the New York State Board of Elections, Eric T. Schneiderman as Attorney General of the State of New York, ~~Kimberley Galvin, Kathleen O'Keefe, Brian D. Rusk, Hilda B. Classon, Marc A. Landis, Jeremy D. Richardson, Scott K. Bailey and Victor Antonio Perez~~,

Defendants

STATE OF NEW YORK :
: SS
COUNTY OF NEW YORK :

The plaintiffs Sam Sloan, Nenad Bach, Geeta Rankoth, Neil V. Grimaldi, Millie Quinones, Trina Jackson, Tiara Lawrence, Nereida Narveaz and Veniada Quinones state:

1. The plaintiffs herein are filing a summons and complaint and are moving by Order to Show Cause bringing a motion for an injunctive relief directing The New York State Board of Elections to place Sam Sloan on the ballot as a Democratic candidate for Governor of New York State, Nenad Bach as Candidate for Lieutenant Governor of New York State, Geeta Rankoth as Candidate for Comptroller of New York

State and Neil V. Grimaldi as Candidate for Attorney General of New York State in the Democratic Primary to be held on September 9, 2014. No prior application has been made in this court for the relief requested herein.

2. The jurisdiction of this court and plaintiffs right to bring this action are found under 42 U.S.C. S 1983, 1988 First Amendment right to political association and Fourteenth Amendment right to due process and equal protection of law.

3. Millie Quinones, Trina Jackson, Tiara Lawrence, Nereida Narveaz and Veniada Quinones are registered voters in the State of New York who wish to vote for these candidates.

4. Brian D. Rusk, Hilda B. Classon, Marc A. Landis, Jeremy D. Richardson, Scott K. Bailey and Victor Antonio Perez are objectors who filed objections with the New York State Board of Elections against Neil V. Grimaldi and Geeta Rankoth. No objections were filed against Sam Sloan or Nenad Bach.

5. The plaintiffs herein seeking this injunctive relief against the government action of removing the name of Sam Sloan on the ballot as a Democratic candidate for Governor of New York State, Nenad Bach as Candidate for Lieutenant Governor of New York State, Geeta Rankoth as Candidate for Comptroller of New York State and Neil V. Grimaldi as Candidate for Attorney General of New York State in the Democratic

Primary to be held on September 9, 2014.

6. The plaintiffs, First Amendment constitutional rights as voters would suffer irreparable harm if these candidates are removed from the ballot.

7. There is a likelihood of success on the merits for the plaintiffs action to seek to put them on the ballot so these voters can exercise their constitutional rights to vote for a candidate of their choice.

8. The election is to be held on September 9, 2014, so the plaintiffs are moving for injunction relief because of the short time in question for them to seek their protected rights under the United States Constitution.

9. If the election were to go forward without the relief requested, this would be an irreparable damage to plaintiffs' constitutional First Amendment right to vote and upon information and belief, the Democratic voters of this 6th Congressional District would have no choice in their primary. It is well known fact that the winner of the Democratic Primary in this District would most likely win the November election.

10. The right for a candidate to appear on the ballot is integral to

the right to vote and is a right protected by the united states constitution.

11. Plaintiffs have no plain or adequate remedy in any other court and timely relief can be obtained by plaintiffs only through the granting of Writ of Mandamus by this court.

12. The Board of Elections of the State of New York on August 1, 2014 illegally violated the rights of each of these candidates by removing their names from the ballot without giving them notice that there would be hearing against them.

13. The Board of Elections was totally unfair as issues involving petitions by these candidates as aforementioned where not even on the calender.

14. Incorporating herein as evidence is the youtube video of these proceedings linked at http://www.elections.ny.gov/2014Meetings.html which shows that they clearly violate the due process clause of the 14th amendment.

15. It is clear from this video that it was not on the calender to remove these candidates from the ballot and these names were not on the list of names read by Commissioner Kellner of candidates to be

removed from the ballot.

16. These candidates were required to be given notice as to the sufficiency and quality of their signatures. This was not done.

17. There was never any objections of specifications filed against Sam Sloan or Nenad Bach and required by NY election law 16-102 and 6-154 which states "the written objection to such petition may be filed within three days after the filing of such party certificate or the making of such party nomination. When such an objection is filed, specifications of the grounds of the objections shall be filed within six days thereafter with the same officer or board and if specifications are not timely filed, the objection shall be null and void."

18. The video illustrates that there was no witness at the hearing as requited by NY state evidence law as to the insufficiency of the petitions.

19. The Board of Elections never even reviewed the petitions.

20. On July 8, 2014, four volumes of petitions were filed nominating Sam Sloan as a Democratic candidate for Governor of New York State, Nenad Bach as Candidate for Lieutenant Governor of New York State,

Geeta Rankoth as Candidate for Comptroller of New York State and Neil V. Grimaldi as Candidate for Attorney General of New York State in the Democratic Primary to be held on September 9, 2014.

21. These petitions have four volumes. Volume 1 starts with page One and ends with page 807. Volume 2 starts with page 1 and ends with page 659. Volume 3 starts on page 1 and ends on page 1197. Volume 4 starts on page 1 and ends on page 1402. Thus there are 807 + 659+ 1197 + 1402 or a total of 4065 page numbers on the petition.

22. These petitions were marked valid as appeared on the Board of Elections website at http://www.elections.ny.gov:8080/reports/rwservlet?cmdkey=whofiled

23. However, on August 4, 2014, nearly one month later, the Board of Elections changed them from valid to invalid.

24. Board of Elections did not have a right to review of the petitions because they had the appearance of validity and there were no specific objections.

25. The so-called specific objections filed against Geeta Rankoth and Neil Grimaldi were not sufficiently specific in that they were not line-by-line objections and lacked the specificity necessary to

review them. Although the objection to Rankoth said that she did not have enough signatures, it did not state how many signatures she had and how many are required. As a result, the Board of Elections did NOT throw these candidates off because of objections and they were not on the list of candidates read by Commissioner Kellner at the meeting on August 1, 2014 who were thrown off because of objections. Rather, Sloan, Bach, Rankoth and Grimaldi were thrown off the ballot at the oral request of Kimberley Galvin, the Republican Party Counsel on the Board of Elections.

26. The New York State Board of Elections violated the equal protection clause and One Man One Vote of the Constitution as clearly specified by the US Supreme court in Baker vs. Carr, 361 US 186, Reynolds vs. Sims, 377 US 533, Board of Estimate of City of New York v. Morris 489 U.S. 688 (1988), Avery v. Midland County, 390 U.S. 474 (1968)

27. By being selective as it is has the same basic constitutional violations as the basis of the board of estimates because one voter in Richmond county has same leverage as a voter in Kings County.

28. The Board of Elections has both executive functions and judicial functions. Baker vs. Carr, 361 US 186, Reynolds vs. Sims, 377 US 533, Board of Estimate of City of New York v. Morris 489 U.S. 688

(1988), Avery v. Midland County, 390 U.S. 474 (1968)

29. The New York State Board of Elections gives equal weight pursuant to Republican Party and Democratic Party voters although there are more hundreds of thousands more Democrats than Republics and violates the constitution not giving to representatives of millions of voters in groups not in existence when state constitution was written giving candidates who got over 50,000 votes party status. Also, more non party voters should have more status than Republicans.

30. All this violates one man one vote

31. Board of Elections operates in basic violation of democratic process in that New York City election inspectors are chosen by the board in a prejudicial way because of their party statue which insures that they are prejudiced. They are expected to vote for the candidates selected by the Republican or Democratic chairman making it virtually impossible for a non selected person to win an election. This violates fundamental fairness and the constitution.

32. This case fundamentally violates the rights to those who signed petitions for the slate of candidates by the way the board of elections has operated as aforementioned.

33. Because the Board of Elections composition is intrinsically violative of the United States Constitution Equal Protection Clause and One Man One Vote it should be jheld unconstitutional as under Board of Estimates vs. Morris, supra because

a) In New York City Richmond has a board member as does the more populace Kings County.

b) The board does not represent minor party voters who have ballot access such as the Gren Party, Independence Party, Conservative Party and Working Families Party.

c) The Board does not have representation for independent votes although they are more numerous than Republican Party voters

d) The New York State Constitution which established representation for the Republican Party and Democratic Party was writen many years ago and does not reflect voting reality nowadays

e) The Board gives equal representation to the Republican Party and the Democratic Party although the Democratic voters are much more numerous

34. The New York State Board of Elections has judicial hearings

deciding which candidates are to be on the ballot and this is violative of procedural due process of the Fourteenth Amendment because the Board is selected by the Republican Party Chairman and the Democratic Party Chairman which makes them inherently prejudiced and unfair.

35. The local boards of elections in New York hires party loyalists as election inspectors who have fraudulently been hired to vote for the chosen party candidates and are not independent inspectors to voting and have acted fraudulently because their paid job depends on their being loyal to the party chairmen of the Republican and Democratic Parties which undermines the fairness of the democratic process and is flagrantly violative of the constitutionally protected elements of fair elections.

WHEREFORE, the plaintiffs seek the following remedy:

1. Sam Sloan be placed on the ballot as a Democratic candidate for Governor of New York State, Nenad Bach as Candidate for Lieutenant Governor of New York State, Geeta Rankoth as Candidate for Comptroller of New York State and Neil V. Grimaldi as Candidate for Attorney General of New York State in the Democratic Primary to be held on September 9, 2014.

2. The New York State Board of Elections should be declared unconstitutional

3. That the attorney for the plaintiffs be paid legal fees for this case

4. That the plaintiffs be paid all the cost of this case.

5. That this court take all such action it deems just and proper.

Dated: Bronx, New York
August 29, 2014

....
Neil Grimaldi, Petitioner
2860 Buhre Avenue, Suite 1E
Bronx, New York 10461

646-229-7974

....
Sam Sloan, Petitioner
1664 Davidson Ave 1B
Bronx, New York 10453

917-507-7226
917-659-3397

STATE OF NEW YORK
COUNTY OF ALBANY

VERIFICATION

Sam Sloan, being duly sworn, deposes and says that he is the plaintiff herein, that he has read the foregoing petition and knows the contents thereof that the same is true as to his own knowledge except as to those matters alleged upon information and belief and as to those matters he believes it to be true.

Sam Sloan

Sworn to before me this 29th
day of August 2014

CUI YING LI
Notary Public, State of New York
No. 01LI6303092
Qualified in New York County
Commission Expires May 12, 2018

Notary Public

STATE OF NEW YORK
COUNTY OF ALBANY

VERIFICATION

Neil V. Grimaldi, being duly sworn, deposes and says that he is the plaintiff herein, that he has read the foregoing petition and knows the contents thereof that the same is true as to his own knowledge except as to those matters alleged upon information and belief and as to those matters he believes it to be true.

Neil V. Grimaldi

Sworn to before me this 29th
day of August 2014

CUI YING LI
Notary Public, State of New York
No. 01LI6303092
Qualified in New York County
Commission Expires May 12, 2018

Notary Public

1:14-CV-1071
MAD/CFH

U.S. DISTRICT COURT
N.D. OF N.Y.
FILED

SEP 02 2014

LAWRENCE K. BAERMAN, CLERK
ALBANY

STATE OF NEW YORK
COUNTY OF NEW YORK

VERIFICATION

Millie Quinones, being duly sworn, deposes and says that he is the plaintiff herein, that he has read the foregoing petition and knows the contents thereof that the same is true as to his own knowledge except as to those matters alleged upon information and belief and as to those matters he believes it to be true.

Millie Quinones
1921 Jerome Ave
Bx, N.Y. 10453

Millie Quinones

Sworn to before me this 29th day of August 2014

CUI YING LI
Notary Public, State of New York
No. 01LI6303092
Qualified in New York County
Commission Expires May 12, 2018

Notary Public

STATE OF NEW YORK
COUNTY OF NEW YORK

VERIFICATION

Tiara Lawrence, being duly sworn, deposes and says that he is the plaintiff herein, that he has read the foregoing petition and knows the contents thereof that the same is true as to his own knowledge except as to those matters alleged upon information and belief and as to those matters he believes it to be true.

Tiara Lawrence

Sworn to before me this 29th
day of August 2014

CUI YING LI
Notary Public, State of New York
No. 01LI6303092
Qualified in New York County
Commission Expires May 12, 2018

Notary Public

STATE OF NEW YORK
COUNTY OF NEW YORK

VERIFICATION

Trina Jackson, being duly sworn, deposes and says that he is the plaintiff herein, that he has read the foregoing petition and knows the contents thereof that the same is true as to his own knowledge except as to those matters alleged upon information and belief and as to those matters he believes it to be true.

Trina Jackson

Sworn to before me this 29th
day of August 2014

CUI YING LI
Notary Public, State of New York
No. 01LI6303092
Qualified in New York County
Commission Expires May 12, 2018

Notary Public

STATE OF NEW YORK
COUNTY OF NEW YORK

VERIFICATION

Nereida Narveaz, being duly sworn, deposes and says that he is the plaintiff herein, that he has read the foregoing petition and knows the contents thereof that the same is true as to his own knowledge except as to those matters alleged upon information and belief and as to those matters he believes it to be true.

Nereida Narveaz

Sworn to before me this 29th
day of August 2014

CUI YING LI
Notary Public, State of New York
No. 01LI6303092
Qualified in New York County
Commission Expires May 12, 2018

Notary Public

STATE OF NEW YORK
COUNTY OF NEW YORK

VERIFICATION

Veniada Quinones, being duly sworn, deposes and says that he is the plaintiff herein, that he has read the foregoing petition and knows the contents thereof that the same is true as to his own knowledge except as to those matters alleged upon information and belief and as to those matters he believes it to be true.

Veniada Quinones

Sworn to before me this 29th
day of August 2014

CUI YING LI
Notary Public, State of New York
No. 01LI6303092
Qualified in New York County
Commission Expires May 12, 2018

Notary Public

AO 440 (Rev. 12/09) Summons in a Civil Action

UNITED STATES DISTRICT COURT

Northern for the New York

Sam Sloan, et al.

Plaintiff

v.

New York State Board of Elections
New York State Attorney General

Defendant

Civil Action No. 1:14CV1071 MAD/CFH

SUMMONS IN A CIVIL ACTION

To: *(Defendant's name and address)*
New York State Board of Election
40 North Pearl St, Albany NY 12207
NY State Attorney General
State Capitol Albany NY

A lawsuit has been filed against you.

Within 21 days after service of this summons on you (not counting the day you received it) — or 60 days if you are the United States or a United States agency, or an officer or employee of the United States described in Fed. R. Civ. P. 12 (a)(2) or (3) — you must serve on the plaintiff an answer to the attached complaint or a motion under Rule 12 of the Federal Rules of Civil Procedure. The answer or motion must be served on the plaintiff or plaintiff's attorney, whose name and address are: Neal Grumfeld, Esq
2860 Buhre Ave 16
Bronx NY 10461
646 229 7974

If you fail to respond, judgment by default will be entered against you for the relief demanded in the complaint. You also must file your answer or motion with the court.

CLERK OF COURT Lawrence K. Baerman

Date: 8/29/2014

Tara Burtt
Signature of Clerk or Deputy Clerk

AO 440 (Rev. 12/09) Summons in a Civil Action

UNITED STATES DISTRICT COURT

for the

Northern District of New York

Sam Sloan, Nenand Bach, Geeta Rankorth, Neil Grimald et al

Plaintiff

v.

New York State Board of Elections and New York Attorney General

Defendant

Civil Action No. 1:14-CV-1071 MAD/CFH

SUMMONS IN A CIVIL ACTION

To: *(Defendant's name and address)* New York State Board of Elections 40 North Pearl St. Albany 12207

New York State Attorney General State Capitol and Robert Abrams Building State Street Albany 12207

A lawsuit has been filed against you.

Within 21 days after service of this summons on you (not counting the day you received it) — or 60 days if you are the United States or a United States agency, or an officer or employee of the United States described in Fed. R. Civ. P. 12 (a)(2) or (3) — you must serve on the plaintiff an answer to the attached complaint or a motion under Rule 12 of the Federal Rules of Civil Procedure. The answer or motion must be served on the plaintiff or plaintiff's attorney, whose name and address are: Neil Grimald Esq. 2860 Buhre Ave 1E The Bronx NY 10461 646 229 7974

If you fail to respond, judgment by default will be entered against you for the relief demanded in the complaint. You also must file your answer or motion with the court.

Lawrence K. Baerman
CLERK OF COURT

Date: 8/29/2014

[signature]
Signature of Clerk or Deputy Clerk

UNITED STATES DISTRICT COURT
NORTHERN DISTRICT OF NEW YORK

1:14-CV-1071 MAD/C

Sam Sloan, Nenad Bach, Geeta Rankoth, Neil V. Grimaldi, Millie Quinones, Trina Jackson, Tiara Lawrence, Nereida Narveaz and Veniada Quinones,

Plaintiffs

ORDER TO SHOW CAUSE

-against-

Douglas A. Kellner, Andrew Spano, James A. Walsh, Gregory P. Peterson, Commissioners and Constituting the New York State Board of Elections, Eric T. Schneiderman as Attorney General of the State of New York, Kimberley Galvin, Kathleen O'Keefe, Brian D. Rusk, Hilda B. Classon, Marc A. Landis, Jeremy D. Richardson, Scott K. Bailey and Victor Antonio Perez,

Defendants

Upon the annexed petition of Neil V. Grimaldi duly verified the 29th day of August, 2014 and the verification of Sam Sloanupon all of the papers and proceedings had herein it is hereby

ORDERED that the Respondents show cause before this court on the Day of , 2014 at M of that day or as soon thereafter as counsel can be heard why an order should not be made and entered herein Restoring Sam Sloan, Nenad Bach, Geeta Rankoth and Neil V. Grimaldi as candidates for election to Governor, Lieutenant Governor, Comptroller and Attorney General

Sufficient Cause appearing therefore, it is further

ORDERED that service of a copy of this order to show cause together with a copy of the papers upon which it is based be served by delivery to the New York State Board of Elections at 40 N. Pearl Street, Albany NY 12207 and upon the Attorney General of the State of New York at the Robert Abrams Building, Albany NY on or before _____ PM on August , 2014 and upon the other respondents by certified mail be deemed good and sufficient service.

ENTER:

____

USDJ

State of New York
Supreme Court, Appellate Division
Third Judicial Department

Decided and Entered: August 21, 2014 519493

In the Matter of SAM SLOAN, as Candidate for Governor of the State of New York, et al.,
Appellants,

v

MEMORANDUM AND ORDER

DOUGLAS A. KELLNER et al., as Commissioners Constituting the New York State Board of Elections, et al.,
Respondents,
et al.,
Respondent.

Calendar Date: August 21, 2014

Before: McCarthy, J.P., Garry, Egan Jr., Lynch and Clark, JJ.

Neil Grimaldi, New York City, for appellants.

Kathleen O'Keefe, New York State Board of Elections, Albany, for Douglas A. Kellner and others, respondents.

Per Curiam.

Appeal from an order and judgment of the Supreme Court (Ceresia, J.), entered August 15, 2014 in Albany County, which dismissed petitioners' application, in a proceeding pursuant to Election Law § 16–102, to declare valid the designating petition naming petitioners Sam Sloan, Nenad Bach and Geeta Rankoth as Democratic Party candidates for certain statewide public offices in the September 9, 2014 primary election.

Petitioners, Sam Sloan, Nenad Bach and Geeta Rankoth, filed a designating petition nominating them as Democratic Party candidates for the respective public offices of Governor, Lieutenant Governor and Comptroller of the State of New York. The designating petition further nominates a nonparty, Neil V. Grimaldi, as Democratic Party candidate for the public office of Attorney General of the State of New York.[1] Objections were filed with regard to the candidacy of Rankoth and asserted, among other things, that the petition contained fewer than one third of the 15,000 signatures required for any of the four candidacies (see Election Law § 6-136 [1]). The New York State Board of Elections agreed and invalidated the designating petition in its entirety. Petitioners thereafter commenced this proceeding seeking a declaration that the State Board's composition is unconstitutional and an order directing that they be included on the primary ballot. Supreme Court dismissed the petition, and petitioners appeal.

We affirm. As Supreme Court properly found, the present proceeding is jurisdictionally defective due to the "failure to name and serve all those who filed objections to the designating petition" (Matter of Gadsen v Board of Elections of City of N.Y., 57 NY2d 751, 752 [1982]; see Matter of Biscone v Scaringe, 59 AD2d 794, 794 [1977], affd 42 NY2d 1075 [1977]).

Assuming without deciding that the above jurisdictional defect only applies to Rankoth – against whose candidacy objections were filed – petitioners also argue that the composition of the State Board does not give equal weight to each voter as required by the Equal Protection Clause of the 14th Amendment to the US Constitution (see Reynolds v Sims, 377 US 533, 560-561 [1964]). They are incorrect, as the underlying principle of one vote per person does not apply to an appointive board, especially where it is charged with administrative duties (see Rosenthal v Board of Educ. of Cent. School Dist. No. 3 of Town of Hempstead, 497 F2d 726, 729 [2d Cir 1974]; see also Hadley v Junior College Dist. of Metropolitan Kansas City, 397 US

---

[1] Grimaldi's application to be added as a petitioner was denied by Supreme Court as untimely.

50, 54 [1970]; Sailors v Board of Educ. of County of Kent, 387 US 105, 111 [1967]; compare Board of Estimate of City of N.Y. v Morris, 489 US 688, 694-696 [1989]). The State Board was thus properly constituted, and was free to hold that the designating petition, which lacked the necessary number of signatures to support any of petitioners' candidacies, was facially defective and invalid in its entirety (see Election Law § 6-154 [1]; Matter of Hunting v Power, 54 Misc 2d 120, 122 [1967], affd 28 AD2d 826 [1967], affd 20 NY2d 680 [1967]).

Petitioners' remaining arguments have been considered and found to lack merit.

McCarthy, J.P., Garry, Egan Jr., Lynch and Clark, JJ., concur.

ORDERED that the order and judgment is affirmed, without costs.

ENTER:

Robert D Mayberger

Robert D. Mayberger
Clerk of the Court

SUPREME COURT OF THE STATE OF NEW YORK
COUNTY OF ALBANY

In the Matter of the Application of Sam Sloan, as Candidate for Governor of the State of New York, Nenad Bach as Candidate for Lieutenant Governor of the State of New York and Geeta Rankoth as Candidate for Comptroller of the State of New York

Petitioners-Candidates-Aggrieved

REPLY BRIEF

-against-

DOUGLAS A. KELLNER, ANDREW SPANO, JAMES A. WALSH and GREGORY P. PETERSON Commissioners and Constituting the NEW YORK STATE BOARD OF ELECTIONS

Respondents

Index No. 4003-14

ERIC T. SCHNEIDERMAN as Attorney General of the State of New York

---

For an Order Pursuant to Sections 16-100, 16-102 and 16-116 of the Election Law Declaring Valid the Designating Petitions purporting to Designate SAM SLOAN, NENAD BACH and GEETA RANKOTH as candidates for the Democratic Party nomination for Governor, Lieutenant Governor and Comptroller of New York State, respectfully at the Primary Election to be held at September 9, 2014 and restoring them to the Official Ballots of Such Primary Election

---

TO THE SUPREME COURT OF THE STATE OF NEW YORK:

COUNTY OF ALBANY

POINT ONE

The Judge's decision failed to differentiate between between an educational administrative body and the New York Board of Elections, which is an executive body with quasi-judicial functions

and decides issues involving the United States Constitutional Rights of Voters to their choice of candidates and the candidate's United States rights.

The Board of Estimates vs. Morris 489 US 688 (1988) governs this case rather than the much earlier decision of Sailors et al vs. Board of Education of Kent et al, 387 US 105 (1967) because the New York State Board of Elections is much more similar to the Board of Estimates of the City of New York and the fact is that the Board of Estimates case is later.

The case of Sailors, supra concerned only the election of county school board members whose electors are elected by the people. Where a school board member has a non-legislative office for which no election is involved or required. The Sailors case required "a subordinate governmental instrumentality created by the state to assist in carrying out of state governmental functions.

The court in Sailors based their decision on the fact that the work done by the Kent County was basically minor.

The Board of Elections of New York has a quasi-judicial functions invalidating candidates from the ballot and this involve decisions regarding United States Constitutional rights of voters and candidate,

Therefore the standard is "one man one vote " is the established law of the nation, Gray v, Saunders 372 U.S. 368, Reynolds v Sims 377 U,S,533; Baker v. Carr 369 U.S.186; Guttney v Cummins 412 U.S. 735; Seaman v Fedourich 16 N.Y. 2d 44; Moder v Ogilve 394 U.S. 814, Oliver v Bd of Education 306 F Supp 1286.

Restraints imposed by the constitution on the states can never be circumvented by local bodies to

whom the state delegates authority like The Board of Elections for the State of New York and the Board of Elections for The City of New York. Standard Computing Scale Company v Farrell 249 U.S. 577; Cooper v Aaron 358 U.S. 1,17.

The other case the judge cited is Cohanim vs. New York City Board of Education, 204 F. Supp. 2d 452, 453 (2002) involved only how New York City Board of Education members are selected. Their Education Board is in no way comparable to the New York State Board of Elections which has quasi-judicial and executive functions regarding the United States Constitutional Rights of voters in having candidates of their choice and the United States Constitutional Rights of candidates.

In Hedley vs. Junior College District, 397 US 50, the United States Supreme Court dispensed with the standard set forth in Sailors, supra and held that the election to a position that performed a governmental function as the New York States Board of Elections does must accord with "one man one vote"

The Fourteenth Amendment section 1 states "nor deny any person within its jurisdiction the equal protection of the law" All voters including members of all other parties other than Republican or Democratic have no voice or representation on the Board of Elections and deprives them of equal protection of the laws. The Board of Estimate v Morris, supra.

The equal protection clause forbids the elevation of a small class of super-voters granted an extraordinary powerful franchise as does the Board of Elections for Republican and Democratic only voters. Brown v Tonson 462 U.S. 835 (1083)

The Board of Elections not representing smaller parties violates minority rights of smaller parties as set forth in Section 2 of The Federal Voting Rights Act 42 U.S. 1973 et seq,

The New York State Board of Elections and their local boards must be held unconstitutional because they fail to represent millions of voters and they violate "one man one vote" Dunn v Blumstein 408 U,S, 330 (1972); Abate v Mundt 403 U.S. 182.

The fact The Board makes quasi-judicial decisions and is made up of members who have an interest in the outcome makes them an unfair judicial body thus violating procedural due process of the Fourteenth Amendment. The Board members chosen by the chairmen of the Republican and Democratic parties is especially prejudicial when they vote on issues of ballot access who are the individuals who appointed them as this slate of candidates including Sam Sloan for Governor has done.

The Board of Elections could not heretofore produce one valid and sustainable legal precedent for the continuation of The Board of Elections in the face of all the existing cases cited herein that prove and illustrates clearly that The Board violates The Equal Protection Clause and "one man one vote"legal precedents that protect individuals like the petition signers and all the candidates that are on this slate as Petitioners .Reynolds v Sims; Connor v. Finch, 431 U.S. 407, 420 (1977); Cohen v Mahoney,410 F. Supp 1286; Grisbaum v. McKeithen, 339 F. Supp. 267 (1971), Latino Political Action Commitee, Inc. vs. City of Boston, 784 F.2d 409 (1986); Iannucci v. Bd. of Supervisors of Washington County, 20 N.Y. 2D 244,249: Franklin v Mandeville ,26 N.Y. 2D 65, 69-70; Franklin v Krause 32 N.Y. 2D 234; Westberry v Sanders 403 U.S. 1; Curcio v Boyle 147 A.D. 194; Jackson v Nassau County Bd. of Supervisors, 818 F. Supp. 98; Very v Midland County 390 U.S. 547, Whitcomb v Chavis 403 U.S. 124,145-146 (1976) Karcher v Daggett, 46 U.S. 725,741

(1971).

POINT TWO

The Supreme Court had insufficient evidence as a matter of law to invalidate these candidates from being on the ballot and violating the United States constitutional rights of their petition signers and The Board of Elections violated procedural due process in invalidating the petitions without notice to the Petioner - Candidates and not having a viable hearing at The Board as required by The Fourteenth Amendment and the due process clause. Goldberg v Kelly;397 U. S. 284; Bell v Bunson 402 U.S. 535, Sherber v Verner, 374 U.S, 374 U.S. 309.

Dated: August 21, 2014
Bronx NY

Respectfully submitted,

Neil Grimaldi

Neil V. Grimaldi
2860 Buhre Ave 1E
Bronx NY 10461

646-229-7974

NEW YORK COURT OF APPEALS

In the Matter of the Application of SAM SLOAN, as Candidate for Governor of the State of New York, NENAD BACH as Candidate for Lieutenant Governor of the State of New York and GEETA RANKOTH as Candidate for Comptroller of the State of New York

Petitioners-Appellants

v

DOUGLAS A. KELLNER, ANDREW SPANO, JAMES A. WALSH and GREGORY P. PETERSON Commissioners and Constituting the NEW YORK STATE BOARD OF ELECTIONS, ERIC T. SCHNEIDERMAN as Attorney General of the State of New York

Respondents-Respondents

LETTER AND MOTION FOR LEAVE TO APPEAL TO THE COURT OF APPEALS

Index No. 4003-14
Third Department Case No. 519493

This proceeding is brought under Election Law Sections 16-100 and 16-102 and other provisions of New York Law. It is well established that under the law of the State of New York including Section 16-102 of Election Law if a candidate files files facially valid petitions and there are no objections filed then the candidate goes on the ballot. There are specific rules about objections in Section 6–154 such as that General Objections must be filed within three days and Specific Objections must be filed within six days more.

Here there were no objections filed as to the candidacies of SAM SLOAN, as Candidate for Governor of the State of New York and NENAD BACH as Candidate for Lieutenant Governor of the State of New

York. The rule based on Section 16-102 of New York Election Law is that if there are no objections to a candidate, his name remains on the ballot. Thus the New York Board of Elections had no jurisdiction to remove Sam Sloan and Nenad Bach from the ballot.

However, there were two identical objections filed as to GEETA RANKOTH as Candidate for Comptroller of the State of New York. Both were identical using even the same printer and font. Those two objections were based in part on the mistaken belief that she was not enrolled in the Democratic Party. She was in fact enrolled in the Democratic Party but the enrollment lists are generally three to four weeks out of date and her name had not yet appeared on the lists. She had enrolled just after turning age 18. There was also an objection as to her age, as the statutory requirement for Comptroller is age 30 and she had not reached that age. There was also a generalized objection as to the number of signatures she had submitted. That objection stated stated in full, "a. The nominating petition fails to contain the minimum number of signatures required by the NYS Election Law for nomination for the public office of Comptroller of the State of New York."

This is all it said. There was nothing more. However, the Appellate Division Third Department wrote, "Objections were filed with regard to the candidacy of Rankoth and asserted, among other things, that the petition contained fewer than one third of the 15,000 signatures required for any of the four candidacies (see Election Law 6-136 [1])."

As you can see, this was not correct neither factually as a statement of law. Neither of the two objectors said that the petition of Geeta Rankoth contained fewer than one-third of 15,000 signatures. They merely stated that they contained less than the required number of signatures, which could be 14,999 signatures for example.

State law does NOT say that the petitions must contain 15,000 signatures. It actually says the petition "must be signed by not less than fifteen thousand or five per centum, whichever is less, of the then enrolled voters of the party in the state (excluding voters in inactive status)". We do not know how many enrolled voters there are in the party and how many are on inactive status. This requires a mathematical calculation. It is not up to us nor up to the Board of Elections to make this calculation. In a small party such as the Working Families Party, only a few hundred signatures may be enough to get on the statewide ballot.

What has happened here is without any objections being filed, neither specific nor general, the staff of the Board of Elections apparently decided to count the signatures. They claim that any time anybody claims that there are not enough signatures, they must start counting the signatures. However, that cannot be the rule because if it was the rule then everybody would claim that their opponent did not have enough signatures, putting the staff of the State Board of Elections to the task of counting all the signatures. The attorney for the Board of Elections, Kathleen O'Keefe, at the hearing before Judge Ceresia, said that any time an objector alleges that there is an insufficient number of signatures, then the Board of Elections must count the signatures and determine their validity. However, this is not the rule. The rule is a candidate cannot be kicked off the ballot for insufficient signatures unless someone has objected to the number of signatures. There are a number of cases that support this. The rule is the Objector must count the signatures and inform the board of elections how many signatures there are. Then the Candidate can do his own count and the matter will be resolved at a hearing. In any event the Board of Elections never does any counting. If it were otherwise, then every objector would routinely allege that the number of signatures is insufficient, requiring the Board of Elections and the tax payers to do all the work.

In the case presented here in court, the Board of Elections filed no opposition papers. Nothing in writing. This led the judge to make several silly errors. He stated, "In This regard, it is noted that even the most

cursory facial review of the designating petitions clearly reveals that they could not possibly contain the necessary 15,000 signatures. That is the last numbered page of the submitted designating petitions is 1402 and each page allotted for no more than 10 signatures. Thus even with 1402 pages with ten signatures on each page would fall approximately 1000 pages short of what was needed."

However, he obviously never looked at the petitions and neither did the Appellate Division because while Volume 4 does contain 1402 pages, there is also volumes 1, 2 and 3. The judge, Andrew G. Ceresia, and the lawyer for the Board of Elections obviously never looked at the petitions because otherwise they would not have made such a stupid remark.

The petition has four volumes

Volume 1 starts with page One and ends with page 807

Volume 2 starts with page 1 and ends with page 659

Volume 3 starts on page 1 and ends on page 1197

Volume 4 starts on page 1 and ends on page 1402

Thus there are 807 + 659+ 1197 + 1402 or a total of 4065 page numbers on the petition.

Here counsel for the Board of Elections engaged in several ethical violations by not informing the judge and the Appellate Division of his mistake and also tampering with the evidence. Counsel for the Board of Elections did not submit the actual petitions to the court. Instead, she submitted what she said were "true and correct" copies. However, they were not true nor were they correct. The original petitions were on thick green petitioning paper 8.5 x 14 and card stock. What she submitted to the court instead was minaturized copies on ultra-thin copy paper. Then she used the small size of what she submitted to make it seem obvious that there were not enough signatures.

The following cross examination took place on pages 27-28 the transcript which is on pages 67-68 of the

record on appeal

(Sam Sloan - Cross by Ms. O'Keefe)

Q Mr. Sloan, are you aware of how many sheets of
paper are in a ream of paper? Are you aware of how many are
in a ream? You buy paper, copy paper in reams?
A I suppose there is 500. I don't know.
Q That's right. And four thousand pages would be how
many reams?
A I guess simple multiplication. It would be eight.
Q It would be eight. Does that stack of pages look
like it's eight reams of paper?
A I'm not an expert on paper size.

It can be seen that she is basing her argument on the size of the stack of paper. The Board of Elections calls this "the weight test". If it appears that the size of the petitions weighs enough, they are not going to inquire further. Here counsel for the Board of Elections did not put the actual petitions on the table. She put minaturized petitions on the table, using copy paper of excessively low bond, not even normal copy paper. Neither the Commissioners of the Board of Elections nor the judge of the Supreme Court saw the actual petitions. The difference was the stack of paper submitted to the court by counsel for the Board of Elections was less than four inches high whereas the actual green petitions are nearly a foot high.

Petitioners counsel made a motion TO SET ASIDE EVIDENCE SUBMITTED BY RESPONDENTS. (See page 36 of the Record) The judge denied the motion, saying that counsel had failed to object to their admission in the proper time and manner. However, the reason counsel did not do so was he had no way to know that the copies of the petitions submitted were vastly different from the originals. Neither the candidates nor their counsel had ever seen the original petitions. It was only hours after the hearing before Judge Ceresia was over and petitioners and counsel were driving back to New York City, that calls were made and counsel found out that the original petitions were submitted on green 8.5 x 14 petitioning paper and card stock, not on the ultra-thin 8.5 x 11 white paper used to make the copies.

At the time of oral argument before the Appellate Division of the Third Department, counsel for the

Board of Elections said that she had given the actual petitions to the appellate court at their request. The court then returned to us the copies we had made at their request, since the originals submitted to the Supreme Court still remain there. Now at this time we do not know what the Appellate Division Third Department had and what this court has. Does it have the minaturized version on white low weight paper or does it have the original petitions on green 8.5 x 14 paper and card stock or does it have both? This uncertainty makes it difficult to argue this appeal.

Counsel for the Board of Elections makes a number of statements about what the Commissioners of the Board of Elections decided. None of these statements are true. For example she says:

> **With respect to that particular candidate, the Board received time specific and general objections from two different objectors. And when the Board met on August 1st the Board voted in public, and they are on a video that's available on YouTube, because they do have their meetings in public, with respect to that candidate, that she did not meet both the signature requirements, as well as the age requirement, and they held her Petition invalid. (See transcript Page 14 in the Record page 54)**

She claims that these statements can be found on youtube. However, none of these statements are on youtube. You need to play the youtube.com video of the meeting on the New York State Board of Elections on August 1, 2014

https://www.youtube.com/watch?v=Soq_8m36RZ0

The important part of the video regarding Sam Sloan, Nanad Bach, Geeta Rakoth and Neil Grimaldi starts at 6:20 and goes on about 20 seconds. There an attorney for the Republican Party, Kimberly Galvin, says she has an addendum to the motion to the board by having Sam Sloan, Nanad Bach, Geeta Rakoth and Neil Grimaldi removed from the ballot. No member of the board mentions those names. Nothing is said by any member of the Board about Geeta Rankoth or anybody else not having enough signatures. No mention is made by anybody about the age requirement to run for Comptroller.

Geeta Rankoth herself had written to the Board stating the following: "I wish to add that it is a violation of federal law to discriminate against me because of my age. Specifically it violates the Age Discrimination in Employment Act of 1967 and other state and federal laws." Neither the Board of Elections nor the Supreme Court nor the Appellate Division were informed of this letter or this issue.

By doing a search on youtube.com for "NYSBOE – 08.01.2014" one can find the actual video of the meeting. Ms. Kathleen O'Keefe is shown on the video, so she was there although she said nothing. Next to her is a man with white hair named Branton. What the video shows is Commissioner Kellner moves to start the agenda with section 4a and then reads off from a sheet of paper a list of 14 candidates and slates who are bring thrown off because of objections. After he finishes reading the list, the Republican Party attorney Kimberly Galvin interrupts by saying that she has an addendum of four names of people she wants thrown off the ballot. She attempts to hand up a sheet that contains the names but is told to read it instead. Those names are Sam Sloan, Nanad Bach, Geeta Rankoth and Neil Grimaldi.

Commissioner Kellner then goes on to read a list of names of candidates who failed to file acceptances and are being thrown off for that reason.

After concluding these lists, Commissioner Kellner states, "We need to make a motion to adopt the Prima Facia list as reported in writing and as I just read."

This is followed by "So Moved" and "Passed".

However, the names of Sam Sloan, Nanad Bach, Geeta Rankoth and Neil Grimaldi were not on the lists "just read" by Commissioner Kellner. Those four names were only mentioned orally by Kimberly Galvin, who is not a member of the board. Neither Commissioner Kellner nor any of the other Commissioners mentioned those names. Therefore, Sam Sloan, Nanad Bach, Geeta Rankoth and Neil Grimaldi were not legally thrown off the ballot.

The judge made another mistake which the Appellate Division adopted when he wrote:

> **"The present proceeding is jurisdictionally defective due to the "failure to name and serve all those who filed objections to the designating petition".**

However, that only applies if the candidate was thrown off because of the objections. Here the candidate is claimed to have been thrown off as a prima facie matter, not because of the objections.

ELECTION LAW § 6–154 states:

> **3. When a determination is made that a certificate or petition is insufficient, such officer or board shall give notice of the determination forthwith by mail to each candidate named in the petition or certificate, and, if the determination is made upon specified objections, the objector shall be notified.**

Here, if Geeta Rankoth was thrown off because of Objections, then the Board was required to notify her and the Objectors "forthwith", BEFORE the meeting of August 1, 2014, to give her time to respond and be heard. The Board did not notify the objectors because Geeta was not thrown off because of Objections. Since Geeta was not thrown off because of Objections and since the Objectors were not notified, there was no obligation to sue the objectors.

In addition, the "Specific Objections" filed against Geeta Rankoth were facially invalid because they were not line by line objections and were not specific enough. A specific objection to the number of signatures is required to state how many signatures there are and how many are required. The rule is the Objector must count the signatures and inform the board of elections how many signatures there are. Then the Candidate can do his own count and the matter will be resolved at a hearing. In any event the Board of Elections never does any counting. This one sentence specific objection in this case does neither. A copy of the two specific objections is attached.

Had these Specific Objections been filed with the New York City Board of Elections rather than the New

York State Board of Elections, they would have been ruled invalid for not being specific enough. This case shows the big differences between the New York City Board of Elections and the New York State Board of Elections, even though they are administered under the same statute. Had this case happened under the New York City Board of Elections, the outcome would have been completely different. Sam Sloan and Nenad Bach would have automatically gotten on the ballot as there were no objections to them. As to Geeta Rankoth, in the absence of line-by-line objections it is not clear what the board would have done but assuming it went to a hearing there would have been a clerk's report following a hearing before the full board in which she would have had an opportunity to defend her petitions.

At the hearing in Albany Supreme Court, a candidate tried to testify as to what was the practice as to the Board of Elections in the City of New York, but this was not allowed. See the transcript of the hearing on page of the transcript in page of the Record:

> **Q There was no evidence filed at the hearing about the inadequacy at the hearing?**
> **A There was no evidence, no even discussion. There**
> **was no discussion about the evidence, how many signatures**
> **there were. They didn't bring out the papers.**
> **I have been to hearings before the Board of**
> **Elections and New York Board of Elections in the City of New**
> **York. And when somebody comes up --**
> **MS. O'KEEFE: Your Honor, objection. The City of**
> **New York is not here before the Court.**
> **THE COURT: Sustained.**

A question concerns the request by Mr. Grimaldi to be added as a petitioner. The reason the petition as filed did not include Mr. Grimaldi is his candidacy was already before Judge McNamara, a different judge in Albany Supreme Court. This case was JOHN CAHILL against NEIL V. GRIMALDI, NO. 3723-14. He naturally thought that his candidacy would be decided in that case and this other case would be duplicative and unnecessary. He was surprised when the Cahill case was dropped. That is why he asked to be added to this case.

Another question concerns documents in the record that Petitioners did not know a bout until the file reached the Appellate Division. These are the Letter of Kathleen O'Keefe dated August 7, 2014 and Exhibits and the Letter of Frank G. Hoare, Esq. dated August 7, 2014 and Exhibits. These are on pages 25-29 of the record. Petitioners did not see any of these documents until they were found in the file at the Appellate Division. They were not marked into evidence and should not have been considered by the Supreme Court or by the Appellate Division.

Petitioners contend that the New York State Board of Elections is an Unconstitutional Body and this case best demonstrates why it is unconstitutional. The New York State Board of Elections consists of four Commissioners. Two are appointed by the State Democratic Party Chairman and the other two are appointed by the State Republican Party Chairman.

The two lawyers fighting this case are Kimberley Galvin, the Republican Party attorney, and Kathleen O'Keefe, the Democratic Party attorney.

Where are the attorneys for the Green, Conservative, Working Families and Independence parties?

Why cannot the millions of voters with no party affiliation be allowed to have some say in who is allowed to run for election?

For all of these reasons we ask that leave to be appeal be granted so these issues can be decided.

Samuel H. Sloan
1664 Davidson Avenue, Apt. 1B
Bronx NY 10453

917-507-7226
917-659-3397
samhsloan@gmail.com

NEW YORK STATE BOARD OF ELECTIONS
40 North Pearl Street, Suite 5
Albany, NY 12207

SPECIFICATION OF OBJECTIONS

TO THE NEW YORK STATE BOARD OF ELECTIONS:

ALLEGED BY OBJECTOR, SCOTT K. BAILEY
(printed name of the objector)

1. I am a registered voter, in the State of New York residing at:

1103 24th Street, Watervliet,
(complete address)

State of New York, 12189.
(zip code)

2. The Nominating Petition filed on behalf of **GEETA RANKOTH** for the public Office of Comptroller of the State of New York for the Primary Election to be held September 9th, 2014, must be ruled void and invalid as and for the following Specifications of Objections:

a. The nominating petition fails to contain the minimum number of signatures required by the NYS Election Law for nomination for the public office of Comptroller of the State of New York;

b. Based on the review of the public record, the purported candidate for the public office of Comptroller of the State of New York, **GEETA RANKOTH**, is not qualified as a candidate as she is younger than the minimum constitutional and statutory age to serve in said public office; and

c. The purported candidate for the public office of Comptroller of the State of New York, **GEETA RANKOTH**, is not eligible to be a candidate in the Democratic Primary to be held on September 9th, 2014 because she is not an enrolled member of the Democratic Party.

The objector reserves the right to raise additional issues at any hearing at which this matter is to be deliberated and determined.

2014 JUL 17 PM 12:

FILED
NEW YORK STATE
BOARD OF ELECTIONS
ALBANY, NEW YORK

[signature]
Objector

07/16/2014
Date

NEW YORK STATE BOARD OF ELECTIONS
40 North Pearl Street, Suite 5
Albany, NY 12207

SPECIFICATION OF OBJECTIONS

TO THE NEW YORK STATE BOARD OF ELECTIONS:

ALLEGED BY OBJECTOR, VICTOR ANTONIO PEREZ
(printed name of the objector)

1. I am a registered voter, in the State of New York residing at:

188 Brinsmade Ave, Bronx
(complete address)

State of New York, 10465.
(zip code)

2. The Nominating Petition filed on behalf of **GEETA RANKOTH** for the public Office of Comptroller of the State of New York for the Primary Election to be held September 9th, 2014, must be ruled void and invalid as and for the following Specifications of Objections:

a. The nominating petition fails to contain the minimum number of signatures required by the NYS Election Law for nomination for the public office of Comptroller of the State of New York;

b. Based on the review of the public record, the purported candidate for the public office of Comptroller of the State of New York, **GEETA RANKOTH**, is not qualified as a candidate as she is younger than the minimum constitutional and statutory age to serve in said public office; and

c. The purported candidate for the public office of Comptroller of the State of New York, **GEETA RANKOTH**, is not eligible to be a candidate in the Democratic Primary to be held on September 9th, 2014 because she is not an enrolled member of the Democratic Party.

The objector reserves the right to raise additional issues at any hearing at which this matter is to be deliberated and determined.

Objector

7-17-14
Date

NEW YORK STATE BOARD OF ELECTIONS
40 North Pearl Street, Suite 5
Albany, NY 12207

SPECIFICATION OF OBJECTIONS

TO THE NEW YORK STATE BOARD OF ELECTIONS:

ALLEGED BY OBJECTOR, VICTOR ANTONIO PEREZ
(printed name of the objector)

1. I am a registered voter, in the State of New York residing at:

188 Brinsmade Ave, Bronx
(complete address)

State of New York, 10465.
(zip code)

2. The Nominating Petition filed on behalf of **GEETA RANKOTH** for the public Office of Comptroller of the State of New York for the Primary Election to be held September 9th, 2014, must be ruled void and invalid as and for the following Specifications of Objections:

a. The nominating petition fails to contain the minimum number of signatures required by the NYS Election Law for nomination for the public office of Comptroller of the State of New York;

b. Based on the review of the public record, the purported candidate for the public office of Comptroller of the State of New York, **GEETA RANKOTH**, is not qualified as a candidate as she is younger than the minimum constitutional and statutory age to serve in said public office; and

c. The purported candidate for the public office of Comptroller of the State of New York, **GEETA RANKOTH**, is not eligible to be a candidate in the Democratic Primary to be held on September 9th, 2014 because she is not an enrolled member of the Democratic Party.

The objector reserves the right to raise additional issues at any hearing at which this matter is to be deliberated and determined.

[signature]
Objector

7-17-14
Date

NEW YORK STATE BOARD OF ELECTIONS
40 North Pearl Street, Suite 5
Albany, NY 12207

SPECIFICATION OF OBJECTIONS

TO THE NEW YORK STATE BOARD OF ELECTIONS:

ALLEGED BY OBJECTOR, SCOTT K. BAILEY
(printed name of the objector)

1. I am a registered voter, in the State of New York residing at:

1103 24th Street, Watervliet,
(complete address)

State of New York, 12189.
(zip code)

2. The Nominating Petition filed on behalf of **GEETA RANKOTH** for the public Office of Comptroller of the State of New York for the Primary Election to be held September 9th, 2014, must be ruled void and invalid as and for the following Specifications of Objections:

a. The nominating petition fails to contain the minimum number of signatures required by the NYS Election Law for nomination for the public office of Comptroller of the State of New York;

b. Based on the review of the public record, the purported candidate for the public office of Comptroller of the State of New York, **GEETA RANKOTH**, is not qualified as a candidate as she is younger than the minimum constitutional and statutory age to serve in said public office; and

c. The purported candidate for the public office of Comptroller of the State of New York, **GEETA RANKOTH**, is not eligible to be a candidate in the Democratic Primary to be held on September 9th, 2014 because she is not an enrolled member of the Democratic Party.

The objector reserves the right to raise additional issues at any hearing at which this matter is to be deliberated and determined.

2014 JUL 17 PM 12:

FILED NEW YORK STATE BOARD OF ELECTIONS ALBANY, NEW YORK

[signature]
Objector

07/16/2014
Date

SUPREME COURT OF THE STATE OF NEW YORK

APPELLATE DIVISION - THIRD DEPARTMENT

In the Matter of the Application of Sam Sloan, as Candidate for Governor of the State of New York, Nenad Bach as Candidate for Lieutenant Governor of the State of New York, Geeta Rankoth as Candidate for Comptroller of the State of New York and Neil v. Grimaldi as Candidate for Attorney General of the State of New York

Petitioners-Candidates-Aggrieved

BRIEF FOR PETITIONERS

-against-

DOUGLAS A. KELLNER, ANDREW SPANO, JAMES A. WALSH and GREGORY P. PETERSON Commissioners and Constituting the NEW YORK STATE BOARD OF ELECTIONS

Index No. 4003-14

Respondents

ERIC T. SCHNEIDERMAN as Attorney General of the State of New York

---

For an Order Pursuant to Sections 16-100, 16-102 and 16-116 of the Election Law Declaring Valid the Designating Petitions purporting to Designate SAM SLOAN, NENAD BACH, GEETA RANKOTH and NEIL V. GRIMALDI as candidates for the Democratic Party nomination for Governor, Lieutenant Governor. Comptroller of New York State and attorney General of New York State respectfully at the Primary Election to be held at September 9, 2014 and restoring them to the Official Ballots of Such Primary Election

---

PRELIMINARY STATEMENT

Petitioners appeal from an August 12, 2014 judgment of the Supreme Court Albany County by Acting Supreme Court Judge Andrew G. Ceresia. By that judgment Petitioner-Appellants were removed from the ballot confirming the ruling by the New York Board of Elections which found petitioners had insufficient signatures.

INTRODUCTION

Petitioners Designating Petitions were filed timely on July 8, 2014. The Board of Elections marked them valid. The case presented at the Supreme Court failed to enter any specifications of objections required by Election Law 16-102 against Sam Sloan, Nenad Bach or Neil V. Grimaldi. There were no specifications of objections entered by Respondent as to insufficient signatures of these candidates.

There were only Specifications of Objections filed against Geeta Rankoth for her insufficient age to be Comptroller which the petitioners accept. However, the petitioners want to replace her through the Committee on Vacancies on the Designating Petitions.

The Petitioners hold that since there were no Objections or Specifications filed against the other candidates they should be permitted to be on the ballot.

There were no Objections or Specifications filed at the Board against Sam Sloan so petitioners argue that there was no basis to exclude him from the ballot. To do so without any notice or a hearing in regard to his petitions violates his Due Process rights under the Fourteenth Amendment.

The court heard of No Specifications or Objections against any other candidate as required by New York Election Law so there is no basis for invalidating their candidacy.

The petitioners hold that the petition signers had United States Constitutional Rights to have candidates of their choices. Their is no basis in this court to invalidate their constitutional rights as federal case law. See Reynolds vs. Sims 377 US 533, Baker vs. Carr, 369 US 186 .

The petitioners herein hold that there were no witnesses called at the Board hearing to justify the invalidating of these designating petitions. The only thing that happened was that an attorney Kimberly Galven stated that we are going to throw off these candidates. Despite the fact that Kimberly Galvin is a paid for the Board of Elections whose office is at 40 North Pearl Street in Albany and only a few blocks from the Supreme Court Albany County at 16 Eagle Street, Miss Galvin was not called as an witness to contradict the testimony of Sam Sloan, a reputable person and mathematician who testified as to his credentials to establish his uncontradicted testimony.

The Board pursuant to Mr. Sam Sloan's uncontradicted testimony violated the due process clause of the Fourteenth Amendment and made a decision without any witnesses. Or falsified based on or even following the basic constitutional requirement of a board as to substantiate their decision. The Board never even examined the designating petitions so even if they try to hold they were insufficient especially without a sworn statement when Miss Galvin was never a sworn witness.

Also the court entered into evidence improperly copies not the original designating petitions. The copies were not even the same size or the same thickness. An examination of the Designating Petitions produced to the court would clearly indicate if they are comparable to that which were entered improperly over objection into evidence.

There was no valid basis at the Board hearing to violate the United States Constitutional rights of the designating petition signers or the candidates on the designating petitions.

Petitioners have sought to invalidate the New York Board of Elections because all the power at the board is given to Republican and Democratic members evenly even though Democrats are more populace than Republicans. Also, the fact that millions of voters who are independent or are members of parties who have no ballot access have no representation on the New York Board of Elections. Also, in New York City, Staten Island has the same amount of representatives, one, as do the more populated boroughs. This was the exact reason specified in Board of Estimate of City of New York v. Morris 489 U.S. 688 (1988) decided: March 22, 1989, that was found to be unconstitutional. This is what the petitioners seek this court to determine.

POINT ONE

The New York State Board of Elections as well as the various city and local county boards should be invalidated pursuant to the law and the ends of justice.

1) In Board of Estimate of City of New York v. Morris 489 U.S. 688 (1988) decided: March 22, 1989, the United States Supreme Court held as I am seeking which is the law of the United States. The United States Supreme Court held the Board of Estimates was illegally constituted because it violated the Equal Protection Clause of the 14th Amendment to the constitution. So, the New York Board of Estimates was found to be null and void as a government agency, citing Reynolds vs. Sims, 377 US 533 and Abate vs Muss, 403 US 182. The Board of Elections completely denies voter equality by ignoring the voting rights of all voters, not Republican or Democrat. Also, Republican Voters have more voting power than Democrats because Democrats far exceed Republican voters. The NY Board of Elections and the New York City Board of Elections violate the Equal Protection Clause based on the disparity between Republicans and Democrats and the fact that so many millions of voters have no representative on the Board of Elections. This inequitable system at the board places the most prejudicial people as executives or board members by how they are chosen by representatives of the Democratic Party

Chairperson and Republican Party Chairperson. Therefore, they cannot constitute a just body or forum to make legal and binding decisions.

This year at a recent July 2014 hearing of the New York City Board of Elections, Eliot Quinones was placed on the ballot by the clerk's report. Then without notice a new Board of Elections clerk's report put him off the ballot. These decisions excluded voters who properly signed the petition. New York Board of Elections clerk's report fundamentally put him off the ballot based on improper decisions excluding voters who properly signed the petition. The New York City Board of Elections also allows one representative and one representative for Brooklyn despite the fact that Brooklyn has three times as many voters as Richmond. This is exactly the reason why the Board of Estimates was found illegal by the United States Supreme Court. The Board of Elections in the City of New York is part of the New York State Board of Elections.

2) Reynolds vs Sims, 377 US 533 established that the Fourteenth Amendment of the United States Constitution established the principle of the equal protection clause and equal protection of the law. Required the Alabama legislature voting to be based on population. The Board of Elections ignores this landmark case and principle. This case stands for the fundamental principle of legislative government in the United States of equal representation for equal numbers of people. The right to vote is a personal right. The idea that one

group can be granted greater voting strength as the board does excluding all Democratic and Republican voters than another is inconsistent with standards for popular representative government. Under the equal protection clause a claim of debasement of the right to vote through mal apportionment represents a practicable controversy. And the equal protection clause provides manageable standards for the lower courts to determine the constitutionality of a state legislative appointment scheme, citing Baker vs. Carr, 361 US 186. In addition it undercuts states voters rights and the duly established United States Constitutional rights.

3) Oliver vs. Board of Education, 306 F. Supp. 1286, No. 69 Civ 2130, United States District Court for the Southern District of New York held that a statute creating the New York City School Board was unconstitutional where the statute provided that citizens of each borough elected one member of the school board. Statute diluted votes of the most populous boroughs. The way the New York State Board of Elections and New York City Board of Elections is organized violates the rights of all voters not Republican or Democratic and gives each Republican voter more power than each Democrat which is unequal and illegal. Also, voting procedures including proxy voting must follow one man one vote Atkins v. Monahan, 91 Misc. 2d 499, 399 NYS 2d 166.

4) Sergey v. King's County Republican Party, 459 F.2d 308 invalidated a county political party's rule on the voting procedure of the one

party where each county committee member has an equal vote weighed according to the number of Republican voters in the district he represents. This violates the one-man one-vote principle established by the Supreme Court as a voters constitutional right. The amount of Democratic Party voters far exceeds the amount of Republican Party voters and gives one Republican and Democratic members equal power and not representing all other voters and Republican or Democratic violated the one-man one-vote constitutional law principle. The equal protection clause applies one man one vote even to count committeemen. Not giving a group the right to representation violates their constitutional rights and discriminates against them. See Moder v. Ogilive 394 US 814, 89 S.Ct. 1493

5) Fisher vs. Board of Supervisors, 59 Misc. 953; 301 NYS 2d 310 citing Seaman v. Fedourich, 16 NY 2d 94, 101 required the "one man one vote" principle required each votes be given equal weight. The Board of Elections excludes the rights of millions of voters and unfairly gives Republican voters more importance than an equal number of Democratic voters. See Burton vs. Schmidt, 128 Misc. 270.

6) The basic exclusion of the Board of Elections of the rights of millions of voters not Republican and Democrat is unequitably a violation of the equal protection clause of the Fourteenth Amendment see Reynolds vs. Sims, supra, Board of Estimates vs. Morris, supra.

7) The New York City Board of Elections has a long history of violating the United States voter's rights and insurgent Democratic and Republican voters rights including none of the other parties by the illegal manner that members of the Board of Elections in New York City as elsewhere are chosen by the New York City Republican and Democratic Party political readers. This violates the Fourteenth Amendment due process requirements because the forum is not a just body and it is constituted in a way by giving undue and improper power to representatives of the Democratic and Republican Chairmen and their representatives who claim to me made a quasi-judicial body making legally binding decisions which they have harmful by their extensive officer and bureau members are selected illegally by the Political Democratic Party Chairmen and Republican Chairmen. It would be proper and legal only to have a civil service Board of Elections. The members of the Board of Elections or an independent non-partisan non-prejudicial system of choosing Board of Election members statewide and in New York City and in each of our great New York County.

8) <u>The Respondents have refused to provide a legal basis in opposition to this motion because there is none.</u>

Whereas Petitioner is requesting an opportunity to subpoena witnesses and present evidence about the long history of political corruption caused by the illegal and improper manner the New York State Board of

Elections and New York City Board of Elections are illegally formed, violative of the equal protection clause one man one vote and basic justice.

POINT TWO

The New York State Board of Elections at their August 1, 2014 meeting and the subsequent Albany Court proceeding on August 11, 2012 were not sufficient to violate the constitutional rights of the Designating Petition signers or the Candidates of their choices or the rights of these candidates to be on the ballot.

The designating petition signers have established and protected United States Constitutional Rights to have the candidates they favor by signing their petition. See Reynolds vs. Sims 377 US 533, Baker vs. Carr, 369 US 186 .

The proceeding at the Board of Elections violates the due process clause of the Fourteenth Amendment rights of these candidates and their designated signers.

1) There was no evidence legally or properly produced to invalidate these petitions.

2) There was no testimony by anyone even Miss Kimberly Galvin

saying we have to throw these designating petitions off the ballot.

3) The board members did not examine the petitions but improperly and illegally based their statement on a paid lawyer representing the Republican party, not a non-partial witness and there was no testimony to justify their actions to violate the US Constitutional Rights of the designating petition voters and their candidates.

4) The court had no basis to allow in minimized copied designating petitions. The respondent Board has said originals and was obligated to produce them. The substitution of these minimized copies from the originals was fraudulent.

CONCLUSION

1) The Board of Elections of the State of New York must be found unconstitutional and eliminated as was the Board of Estimates of the City of New York by the United States Supreme Court and for the same factual and legal reasons.

2) The board failed to properly give consideration failing to require Objections and Specifications and failed to provide Fourteenth Amendment due process of law. They violated the United States Constitutional Rights to due process of law.

Respectfully Submitted,

DATED: August 14, 2014

Bronx, New York

Neil Grimaldi, Esq.

Attorney for Petitioners-Candidates

2860 Buhre Avenue, 1E

Bronx NY 10461

646-229-7974

STATE OF NEW YORK
SUPREME COURT COUNTY OF ALBANY

In the Matter of the Application of
SAM SLOAN, as Candidate for Governor of the State of New York, NENAD BACH, as Candidate for Lieutenant Governor of the State of New York, and GEETA RANKOTH, as Candidate for Comptroller of the State of New York,

Petitioners,

-against-

DECISION/ORDER/ JUDGMENT

DOUGLAS A. KELLNER, ANDREW SPANO, JAMES A. WALSH, and GREGORY P. PETERSON, Commissioners and Constituting the NEW YORK STATE BOARD OF ELECTIONS, and ERIC T. SCHNEIDERMAN, Attorney General of the State of New York,

Respondents.

All Purpose Term
Hon. Andrew G. Ceresia, Acting Supreme Court Justice
Index No. 4003-14

Appearances:[1]

Neil Grimaldi, Esq.
Attorney for Petitioners
2860 Buhre Avenue
Bronx, New York 10461

Kathleen O'Keefe, Esq.
For Respondent New York State
Board of Elections
40 North Pearl Street
Albany, New York 12207-2108

1 Although the Attorney General was a named respondent and was served with the petition, that office advised the Court that it would not be participating in this matter.

Ceresia, J.

Petitioners, arguing that respondent New York State Board of Elections (hereinafter "the Board") improperly invalidated their designating petitions as Democratic Party candidates for statewide offices, commenced the above-captioned proceeding pursuant to Election Law § 16-100 *et seq.* to validate their designating petitions. Petitioners also seek to have the Board declared null and void as violative of the federal constitution and federal law. Finally, petitioners seek attorney's fees. The Board opposed, asserting that petitioners' designating petitions were invalidated because they contained fewer than the minimum number of required signatures, and because petitioner Geeta Rankoth was found not to be of the minimum age required to hold the office of Comptroller.

The Court held a hearing on August 11, 2014, for the purpose of allowing the parties to be heard further and/or present evidence. Petitioners elicited sworn testimony from petitioner Sam Sloan, without objection from the Board. The Board offered into evidence copies of two sets of general and specific objections by Victor Perez and Scott Bailey (Exhibits 2 and 3, respectively), copies of petitioners' designating petitions (Exhibit 4), and a certification indicating that the aforementioned documents were true and exact copies of the originals (Exhibit 1). Petitioners asserted specific objections to the admission of these documents, arguing that the documents should not come into evidence because the Board is unconstitutionally organized and was without authority to act in the absence of objections. Petitioners, however, did not raise any foundational objections or any other objections impacting the admissibility of the documents. As such, the Court overruled petitioners' objections – which, again, bore no relevance to the actual admissibility of the documents in question – and received the exhibits into evidence.[2]

Turning first to the candidacy of Grimaldi -- petitioners' counsel, who seeks to run for the office of New York State Attorney General – it is noted that Grimaldi was not named as a party in the petition commencing this proceeding. Rather, in the same affidavit/motion which set forth petitioners' best evidence objection, petitioners also for the first time seek to add Grimaldi as a named petitioner. Noting that the return date in this matter has passed and the hearing has already been concluded, this application is denied as untimely. In any event, even if Grimaldi were to be added as a named petitioner, he still would not be entitled to the relief that he seeks, for the same reasons set forth below with respect to petitioners Sam Sloan and Nenad Bach.

2

On August 12, 2014, the day after the hearing was concluded, petitioners faxed to the Court an unsworn affidavit/motion from Neil Grimaldi, Esq. No indication has been provided to the Court that said affidavit/motion was served on respondents. Pursuant to the affidavit/motion, petitioners argue for the first time that the best evidence rule prohibited admission into evidence of copies of the designating petitions (Exhibit 4). This objection is untimely. In that regard, the Court notes that, had that objection been raised in a timely manner during the hearing as it was required to be, the Board would have had the chance to be heard on the matter, the Court would have had the opportunity to make a ruling, and the Board ultimately would have had the chance to cure the defect, if any. Accordingly, the petitioners' untimely best evidence objection is now overruled.

Next, with respect to the candidacy of Geeta Rankoth, the instant petition is jurisdictionally defective because, although objections were filed to Rankoth's designating petitions, Rankoth failed to name and serve the objectors, who are necessary parties to a proceeding to validate designating petitions (see Matter of Gadsen v Bd. of Elec. of City of N.Y., 57 NY2d 751, 752 [1982]; Matter of Plochocki v Onondaga County Board of Elections, 21 AD3d 710, 710 [2005]; Matter of Fusco v Westchester County Bd. of Elec., 286 AD2d 456, 456-457 [2001], lv denied 96 NY2d 718 [2001]). Nevertheless, even considering the merits of the petition as it relates to Rankoth, the Board properly ruled that Rankoth's designating petitions were invalid because Rankoth did not meet the age requirement to hold the office of New York State Comptroller, and because her designating petitions contained fewer than the minimum number of signatures. Petitioners concede that Rankoth is too young for the position, and the record reveals that Rankoth's designating petitions contained only 4,087 signatures, far short of the necessary 15,000 (see Election Law § 6-136 [1]). Therefore, the instant petition is denied as it pertains to Rankoth.

With regard to petitioners' further argument that Rankoth should be replaced by a committee on vacancies rather than having her petitions invalidated, "a designated committee to fill vacancies may act only if the designating petition itself is deemed valid" (Matter of Elgin v Smith, 10 AD3d 483, 484 [2004]; see Matter of Owens v Sharpton, 45 NY2d 794, 795 [1978]; Matter of Marcatante v Lundy, 8 Misc 2d 313, 316-317 [1957], affd 4 AD2d 883 [1957]). Here, since Rankoth's designating petitions were invalid, the committee on vacancies is not empowered to name a replacement candidate.

Turning to the candidacies of Sloan and Bach, petitioners claim that the Board acted beyond the scope of its authority and in an arbitrary and capricious manner by invalidating their designating petitions without any objections having been filed. However, under Election Law § 6-154 (1), the Board has the authority to perform a ministerial, facial review of designating petitions to determine whether they are in the proper form and appear to bear the requisite number of signatures (see Matter of Rosen v McNab, 25 NY2d 798, 799 [1969]; Matter of Mansfield v Epstein, 5 NY2d 70, 73 [1958]). The Board may make such a determination even in the absence of objections (see Casler v Bd. of Elec. of Herkimer County, 131 Misc 744, 746 [1928]; see also Jerry H. Goldfeder, Goldfeder's Modern Election Law § 4 [C], at 37; 50 NY Jur 2d Elections § 371). Here, the Board acted properly in conducting a facial review of the designating petitions and then invalidating said petitions on the basis that they did not contain the requisite number of signatures. In that regard, it is noted that even the most cursory facial review of the designating petitions clearly reveals that they could not possibly contain the necessary 15,000 signatures. That is, the last numbered page of the submitted designating petitions was 1,402, and each page allotted for no more than 10 signatures. Thus, even 1,402 pages with 10 signatures on each page would fall approximately 1,000 signatures short of what was needed. Further, there are numerous and significant gaps in pagination such that it is clear that there were significantly fewer than 1,402 pages of designating petitions filed. In addition to that, numerous pages contain fewer than the full allotment of 10 signatures. Therefore, it is clear that the Board acted well within the scope of its authority, was not arbitrary or capricious, and properly invalidated the designating petitions for lack of signatures, even in the absence of objections. Accordingly, the instant petition is denied with respect to Sloan and Bach.

As a final matter, petitioners argue that the composition of the Board violates the federal constitution and federal law because it is made up only of Democrats and Republicans, with no representation by independent voters or minor party members, and thus violates the "one man, one vote" principle. However, "[s]ince the choice of members of the [Board] did not involve an election and since none was required for these nonlegislative offices, the principle of 'one man, one vote' has no relevancy" (Sailors v Bd. of Ed. of Kent County, 387 US 105, 111 [1967]; see Cohanim v New York City Bd. of Ed., 204 F Supp 2d 452, 453 [2002] [holding that the "one person, one vote" standard does not apply to appointed bodies]). As such, petitioners' claim in this regard is without merit.

Accordingly, it is hereby

ORDERED AND ADJUDGED that the petition is denied.

This shall constitute the decision and order of the Court. The original decision and order is returned to the attorney for BOE. All other papers are being delivered to the Supreme Court Clerk for delivery to the County Clerk or directly to the County Clerk for filing. The signing of this decision and order and delivery of this decision and order does not constitute entry or filing under CPLR Rule 2220. Counsel is not relieved from the applicable provisions of that rule respecting filing, entry and notice of entry.

DATED: August 12, 2014
Troy, New York

Andrew G. Ceresia
Acting Supreme Court Justice

Papers Considered:

1. Verified Petition dated August 4, 2014;
2. Letter of Helena Lynch, Esq., dated August 6, 2014;
3. Letter of Kathleen O'Keefe, Esq., dated August 7, 2014, and Exhibits;
4. Letter of Frank G. Hoare, Esq., dated August 7, 2014, and Exhibits.
5. Statement of Law of Neil Grimaldi, Esq., dated August 8, 2014;
6. Affidavit/Motion of Neil Grimaldi, Esq., dated August 11, 2014, received August 12, 2014.

At a Special Term of The Supreme Court of the State of New York, held in and for the County of Albany, at the Supreme Courthouse thereof, on the 4th day of August, 2014

PRESENT: Gerald W. Connolly
HON:

In the Matter of the Application of Sam Sloan, as Candidate for Governor of the State of New York, Nenad Bach as Candidate for Lieutenant Governor of the State of New York and Geeta Rankoth as Candidate for Comptroller of the State of New York

Petitioners-Candidates-Aggrieved

-against-

DOUGLAS A. KELLNER, ANDREW SPANO, JAMES A. WALSH and GREGORY P. PETERSON Commissioners and Constituting the NEW YORK STATE BOARD OF ELECTIONS
Respondents

ERIC T. SCHNEIDERMAN as Attorney General of the State of New York

ORDER TO SHOW CAUSE
TO VALIDATE
DESIGNATING PETITIONS
Index No.
4003-14

For an Order Pursuant to Sections 16-100, 16-102 and 16-116 of the Election Law Declaring Valid the Designating Petitions purporting to Designate SAM SLOAN, NENAD BACH and GEETA RANKOTH as candidates for the Democratic Party nomination for Governor, Lieutenant Governor and Comptroller of New York State, respectfully at the Primary Election to be held at September 9, 2014 and restoring them to the Official Ballots of Such Primary Election

14 AUG -4 PM 4:21
ALBANY, NY

NEW YORK STATE
BOARD OF ELECTIONS
2014 AUG -4 PM 4:43
FILED

Upon the annexed verified petition of Neil Grimaldi and Sam

Sloan duly verified the 4th day of August, 2014 and upon the original Democratic Party designating petitions purporting to designate Sam Sloan as Candidate for the Democratic Party nomination for Governor, Nenad Bach as Candidate for the Democratic Party nomination for Lieutenant Governor and Geeta Rankoth as Candidate for the Democratic Party nomination for Comptroller of New York State respectfully and upon all of the papers and proceedings had herein:

LET the Respondents named herein above show cause before this court at a Special Term for Election Proceedings at be held at the A;bany County and Supreme Court Courthouse, 16 Eagle Street, Albany New York on the 7th day of August, 2014 at 2:00 ~~AM~~ P.M. of that day or as soon thereafter as counsel can be heard why an order should not be made and entered herein: *Personal Appearance Required GWC 8/4/14

1. Declaring sufficient and valid the designating petitions filed with the New York State Board of Elections purporting to designate and/or nominate Sam Sloan as Candidate for the Democratic Party nomination for Governor, Nenad Bach as Candidate for the Democratic Party nomination for Lieutenant Governor and Geeta Rankoth as Candidate for the Democratic Party nomination for Comptroller of New York State to be held on September 9, 2014 and

2. Ordering and decreeing and directing the New York State Board of Elections to restore the names of Sam Sloan,

7

Nenad Bach and Geeta Rankoth to the ballot as Candidates for the Democratic Party nomination for Governor, Lieutenant Governor and Comptroller of New York State to be printed and placed on the official ballots to be used either at the September 9, 2014 Democratic Primary Election and the November 4, 2014 General Election and why the Petitioners should not have such other and further relief as to this court may seem just and proper.

SUFFICIENT CAUSE APPEARING THEREFOR, it is ordered that service of a copy of this order together with a copy of the papers upon which it is based by delivery to the Board of Elections of the state of New York at 40 N. Pearl Street, Suite 5, Albany New York 12207 or by mailing it to their offices at the above address on or before the 3rd day of August 2014 and service of this order on the office of Eric T. Schneiderman as Attorney General of the State of New York before the 5th day of August 2014 be deemed good and sufficient service.

ENTER:

Gerald W. Connolly

HON. Gerald W. Connolly
JUSTICE OF THE SUPREME COURT
OF THE STATE OF NEW YORK

C

SUPREME COURT OF THE STATE OF NEW YORK
COUNTY OF ALBANY

In the Matter of the Application of Sam Sloan, as Candidate for Governor of the State of New York, Nenad Bach as Candidate for Lieutenant Governor of the State of New York and Geeta Rankoth as Candidate for Comptroller of the State of New York

Petitioners-Candidates-Aggrieved

-against-

DOUGLAS A. KELLNER, ANDREW SPANO, JAMES A. WALSH and GREGORY P. PETERSON Commissioners and Constituting the NEW YORK STATE BOARD OF ELECTIONS

Respondents

ERIC T. SCHNEIDERMAN as Attorney General of the State of New York

PETITION TO VALIDATE DESIGNATING PETITIONS
Index No.
4003-14

For an Order Pursuant to Sections 16-100, 16-102 and 16-116 of the Election Law Declaring Valid the Designating Petitions purporting to Designate SAM SLOAN, NENAD BACH and GEETA RANKOTH as candidates for the Democratic Party nomination for Governor, Lieutenant Governor and Comptroller of New York State, respectfully at the Primary Election to be held at September 9, 2014 and restoring them to the Official Ballots of Such Primary Election

---

TO THE SUPREME COURT OF THE STATE OF NEW YORK:

COUNTY OF ALBANY

Your Petitioners by and through their attorney Neil Grimaldi by verified petition respectfully shows and alleges to this court.

1. That at all of the times hereinafter mentioned Sam Sloan, Candidate for the Democratic Party nomination for Governor, Nenad Bach Candidate for the Democratic Party nomination for Lieutenant Governor and Geeta Rankoth Candidate for the Democratic Party nomination for Comptroller of New York State are attempting to be candidates for the Democratic Party at the primary election to be held on September 9, 2014.

2. That at all times hereinafter mentioned the respondent New York State Board of Elections was and is charged with the responsibility of the supervision of the conduct of elections held in New York State including the duties of receiving and filing designating petitions for statewide public office and review and determination of objections and specifications of objections to such designating petitions, nullification of a determination of non-compliance, maintaining the permanent personal voter registration poll records of voters and the preparation of official Primary Election and General Election ballots for use in New York State Elections.

3. That on or about July 8, 2014 there were filed with the New York State Board of Elections certain papers allegedly constituting petitions purporting to designate for the September 9, 2014 Democratic Party Primary Election Sam Sloan, Candidate for the Democratic Party nomination for Governor, Nenad Bach Candidate for the Democratic Party nomination for Lieutenant Governor and Geeta Rankoth Candidate for the Democratic Party nomination for Comptroller of New York State. These petitions included more than 4000 numbered pages and were facially valid and regular with a cover sheet consistent with New York Election Law and the Rules of the Board of Elections of the State of New York..

4. Upon information and belief the said New York State Board of Elections improperly illegally and in

violation of the United States Constitution 14th Amendment due process clause and under the New York State Constitution at an official meeting on August 1, 2014 threw them off the ballot without ever informing Sam Sloan, Candidate for the Democratic Party nomination for Governor, Nenad Bach Candidate for the Democratic Party nomination for Lieutenant Governor and Geeta Rankoth Candidate for the Democratic Party nomination for Comptroller of New York State that there would be a hearing and determination of the validity of their petitions and the possibility of their signatures being invalidated.

5. The Comptroller Candidate Geeta Rankoth is 18 years of age and the law requires that the Comptroller be thirty years old. The Petitioners are seeking to have her replaced by the Committee on Vacancies, and not excluding these petitioners from having a candidate for Comptroller that represents the rights and duties of the designating petition which are to be respected and the practical viewpoints of the designating petition signers who have protected rights to have candidates of their choices.

6. New York State Election Law required that the candidates Sam Sloan, Nenad Bach and Geeta Rankoth have Objections filed against them for inadequate, improper or insufficient signatures before the Board invalidated the designating petitions under United States Law and the United States Constitution.

7. This was not done. Therefore there was no basis for the Board of Elections to invalidate their petitions, especially without giving them adequate notice as required by the United States Constitution 14th Amendment due process clause and New York Election Law and the required and regular procedures of the Board of Elections and the rules of the Board of Elections of the State of New York.

8. New York State election Law requires that a person who files Objections to the nominating petitions

of a candidate file within 6 days Specifications of their Objections; This was not done against the candidates Sam Sloan and Nenad Bach and Geeta Rankoth for inadequate signatures or improperly filed signatures other than the fact that the girl was 18 years old and therefore unqualified to be comptroller and the said attempts these candidates petitions and candidacy.

9. Since there were no proper Objections or Specifications of Objections and the fact that the cover sheet was in proper order as required by New York Election Law, the Board of Elections acted in a arbitrary and capricious manner in violation of the CPLR Article 78 and therefore their actions to invalidate the petitions of these candidates must be held null and void, especially in light of the fact that these three candidates, Sam Sloan, Nenad Bach and Geeta Rankoth never received notice as required by the due process clause of the Fourteenth Amendment that on Friday August 1, 2014 the New York State Board of Elections would consider the possibility of removing them from the ballot.

10. Had the Board of Elections properly informed Sam Sloan, Nenad Bach and Geeta Rankoth, they would have had an opportunity to defend their petitions, an opportunity which was illegally and unfairly denied them and as a violation of the due process clause of the 14th amendment because the hearings were unjust and because these candidates were required to be given notice under the United States Constitution 14th Amendment due process clause and New York Election Law and the rules and regulations and normal procedures followed by the New York Board of Elections.

11. The Democratic process requires that the voters have a choice of different candidates in the primaries. If Geeta Rankoth is excluded as a candidate there is no opponent for comptroller for Thomas P. DiNapoli.

12. The Board of Elections in the State of New York is intrinsically an unfair body in that they are

constituted in being selected by the two major parties , the Republican Party and the Democratic Party and this is so improper that the clients could not get a fair hearing. The fact that the Board of Elections is unfairly constituted warrants that the Board of Elections be deemed violative of the due process clause of the 14th Amendment and they should be disbanded and invalidated. Independent voters in the state of New York have no representation on the New York State Board of Elections. This is unfair because they constitute a larger group than the Republican Party.

13. It is intrinsically violative of the United States Constitution and the one-man-one-vote principle of federal election law makes it unconstitutional that the State Board of Elections does not include representatives of the other parties with ballot access, including the Green Party voters, Conservative Party voters, Independence Party voters and Working Families Party voters. Reynolds vs. Sims 377 US 533 established that the principle of the Equal Protection Clause and equal protection of the law required legislative voting to be based on population. The Board of Elections ignores this landmark case and principle. This case stands for the fundamental principle of representative government in the United States and is one for equal protection for equal number of people. The right to vote is a personal right and the idea that one group can be granted greater voting strength as the board does in excluding all not-Democratic and all non-Republican voters is hostile to the standards to popular representative government. Under the equal protection clause a claim of debasement of the right to vote through malapportionment presents a practicable controversy and the equal protection clause provides manageable standards for the lower courts to determine the constitutionality of state legislative approtionment.. Baker vs. Carr 369 US 186. See also Oliver vs. Board of Education, 306 F. Supp 1286, Atkins vs. Monahan, 91 Misc. 2d 499, 399 NYS 2d 166, Morris vs Board of Supervisors 50 Misc. 2d 929, 273 NYS 2d 453, Sergey v. King's County Republican Party 459 F.2d 308, See Morder v. Ogrlive 394 US 814, 89 S.Ct. 1493

WHEREFORE it is respectfully prayed that this court:

1. Declare sufficient and valid the designating petitions filed with the New York State Board of Elections purporting to designate and/or nominate Sam Sloan as Candidate for the Democratic Party nomination for Governor, Nenad Bach as Candidate for the Democratic Party nomination for Lieutenant Governor and Geeta Rankoth as Candidate for the Democratic Party nomination for Comptroller of New York State to be held on September 9, 2014 and

2. Order and decree and direct the New York State Board of Elections to restore the names of Sam Sloan, Nenad Bach and Geeta Rankoth to the ballot as Candidates for the Democratic Party nomination for Governor, Lieutenant Governor and Comptroller of New York State to be printed and placed on the official ballots to be used either at the September 9, 2014 Democratic Primary Election and the November 4, 2014 General Election and why the Petitioners should not have such other and further relief as to this curt may seem just and proper.

3. Petitioners seek to have the New York Board of Elections as presently organized and constituted declared null and void as violative of the United States Constitution and state and federal laws including the one-man-one-vote principle of the United States Constitution and federal law.

4. Award Petitioners Attorney's Fees

Respectfully Submitted,

Neil Grimaldi
Attorney for Candidates
2860 Buhre Avenue
Bronx NY 10461

646-229-7974

Sam Sloan

Candidate for New York Governor

STATE OF NEW YORK)
) ss:
COUNTY OF ALBANY)

VERIFICATION

I, the undersigned, the petitioner named in the foregoing petition, being duly sworn, says:

I have read the foregoing petition subscribed by me and know the contents thereof and the same is true of my own knowledge, except as to those matters herein stated to be alleged upon information and belief and as to those matters I believe it to be true.

Sam Sloan

On the 4th Day of August, 2014 before me personally came Samuel H. Sloan to me known to be the person described herein and who executed the foregoing instrument. Such person duly swore to such instrument before me and duly acknowledged that he executed the same.

Sheila Horton
NOTARY PUBLIC

SHEILA HORTON
Notary Public, State of New York
Qualified in Albany County
No. 01HO6153076
Commission Expires 9-20-2014

STATE OF NEW YORK)
) ss:
COUNTY OF ALBANY)

ATTORNEY'S VERIFICATION

Neil Grimaldi, an attorney duly admitted to the practice of law before the courts of New York does hereby affirm under penalties of perjury:

1. He is the attorney for the petitioners in this action.

2. He has reviewed the contents of this document with his clients and upon the conclusion of said review as to the facts herein believes the be the same to be true.

3. This affirmation is being used pursuant to the provisions of the CPLR and applicable case law due to the fact that time is of the essence and the petitioner and his counsel are in different counties. Counsel having officer in the county of Bronx and Petitioners residing in a county other than the county of the Bronx.

Neil Grimaldi
Attorney for Petitioners-Candidates
2860 Buhre Avenue
Bronx NY 10461
646-229-7974

On the 4th Day of August, 2014 before me personally came Neil V. Grimaldi to me known to be the person described herein and who executed the foregoing instrument. Such person duly swore to such instrument before me and duly acknowledged that he executed the same.

NOTARY PUBLIC

SHEILA HORTON
Notary Public, State of New York
Qualified in Albany County
No. 01HO6153076
Commission Expires 9-20-2014

STATE OF NEW YORK
OFFICE OF THE ATTORNEY GENERAL

ERIC T. SCHNEIDERMAN
ATTORNEY GENERAL

DIVISION OF STATE COUNSEL
LITIGATION BUREAU

Writer Direct: (518) 408-2009

August 6, 2014

Via Facsimile

The Honorable Andrew G. Ceresia
Justice of the Supreme Court
Supreme Court
County of Albany
16 Eagle Street
New York, New York 12207

Re: <u>Sloan v. Kellner</u>
Index No. 4003-2014
OAG No. 14-172547

Dear Justice Ceresia:

This Office hereby acknowledges receipt of the papers forwarded to us in the above-referenced matter pursuant to the notice requirements of Executive Law § 71 and C.P.L.R. 1012(b)(1) because there appears to be a purported constitutional challenge to a State statute.

Please be advised that, after careful consideration, this Office has determined that we will not be participating in the above-referenced matter at this time. Because there are many reasons why the Office of the Attorney General may decide not to participate, we respectfully suggest that no adverse inference regarding our view of the merits of the constitutional challenge to the State statute, or the nature of the State's interest, should be drawn from our non-participation at this stage.

This Office may choose to intervene at a later stage for purposes of defending the constitutionality of the statute. We note that, pursuant to Executive Law § 71 and C.P.L.R. 1012(b)(1), if this matter is appealed, the Office of the Attorney General must receive another notification of the constitutional challenge. We also would appreciate being advised of any final decision.

Thank you. I can be reached at (518) 408-2009 with any questions.

Respectfully submitted,

HELENA LYNCH
Assistant Attorney General

cc: Neil Grimaldi, Esq. (via United States First Class Mail)
Attorney for Petitioners
2860 Buhre Avenue
Bronx, New York 10461

21

STATE BOARD OF ELECTIONS

40 N. PEARL STREET
ALBANY, N.Y. 12207-2108
Phone: 518/474-2063 Fax: 518/486-6627
www.elections.ny.gov

August 7, 2014

AUG - 7 2014

Hon. Andrew G. Ceresia
Rensselaer County Courthouse
Troy, New York 12180

Via Facsimile Only: (518) 271-1047

Re: *Matter of Sloan, et al v New York State Board of Elections* (Index No: 4003-14)

Dear Judge Ceresia:

The State Board of Elections received a designating petition purporting to designate Sam Sloan a candidate of the Democratic Party for the office of Governor of the State of New York, Nenad Bach a candidate of the Democratic Party for the office of Lt. Governor of the State of New York, Neil V. Grimaldi a candidate of the Democratic Party for the office of New York State Attorney General and Geeta Rankoth a candidate of the Democratic Party for the office of New York State Comptroller.

Subsequently, General Objections and Specifications of Objections were filed by three different objectors with respect to the petition for Neil V. Grimaldi. One objector stated that the candidate claimed 5,113 signatures and that the actual number of valid signatures was zero. The second objector claimed that the petition contains 4,476 signatures, far short of the 15,000 needed. The third objector claimed that the petition does not contain the minimum number of signatures required and fails to contain signatures from one half of the congressional districts in the state as required.

In addition, General Objections and Specifications of Objections were filed by two objectors with respect to the petition for Geeta Rankoth. Both objectors claimed that the petition fails to contain the minimum number of signatures required, that the candidate does not meet the age requirement to hold the office, and that the candidate is not an enrolled member of the Democratic Party.

The Commissioners of the State Board met on August 1, 2014, at which time they made the determination that 4,087 signatures were filed and, therefore, the petition did not contain the 15,000 signatures required to secure the designations in question. The Board also determined that Geeta Rankoth did not meet the age requirement to hold the office of New York State Comptroller. By a unanimous vote of the Board the petitions for all four candidates were held invalid. (See attached Determinations.)

Subsequent to the Board's Determination, this proceeding to validate the designating petition was commenced in Albany Supreme Court. Notably, a separate proceeding to invalidate the designating petition of all four candidates was commenced in Albany Supreme Court on July 18, 2014 (*Cahill v Grimaldi, et al* [Index No. 3723-14]) and was returnable on August 4, 2014 before the Honorable Thomas J. McNamara. My understanding is that the *Cahill* matter was adjourned until today at 2:00 p.m.

Very truly yours,

Kathleen O'Keefe

Kathleen O'Keefe

Cc: Hon. Thomas J. McNamara
Via Facsimile Only: (518) 583-5335

Neil Grimaldi, Esq.
2860 Buhre Avenue
Bronx, NY 10461

FWC

FEATHERSTONHAUGH, WILEY & CLYNE, LLP
ATTORNEYS AND COUNSELLORS AT LAW

99 PINE STREET
ALBANY, NEW YORK 12207
WEBSITE: FWC-LAW.COM

AUG -7 2014

FRANK G HOARE
fgh@fwc-law.com

PHONE: (518) 436-0786
FAX: (518) 427-0452

August 7, 2014

Hon. Andrew G. Ceresia
Rensselaer County Courthouse
Troy, New York 12180

Via Facsimile Only: (518) 271-1047

Re: Matter of Sloan, et al v New York State Board of Elections (Index No: 4003-14)

Dear Judge Ceresia:

I am the attorney for New York State Comptroller Thomas DiNapoli. Comptroller DiNapoli was designated a candidate for the public office of Comptroller of the State of New York at a meeting of the Democratic State Committee on May 21, 2014. (See Certificate of Designation attached hereto).

I write in regard to the designating petition purporting to designate Sam Sloan a candidate of the Democratic Party for the office of Governor of the State of New York, Nenad Bach a candidate of the Democratic Party for the office of Lt. Governor of the State of New York, Neil V. Grimaldi a candidate of the Democratic Party for the office of New York State Attorney General and Geeta Rankoth a candidate of the Democratic Party for the office of New York State Comptroller.

General Objections and Specifications of Objections were timely filed by two objectors, Scott K. Bailey and Victor Antonio Perez with respect to the petition for Geeta Rankoth. Both objectors claimed that the petition fails to contain the minimum number of signatures required, that the candidate does not meet the age requirement to hold the office, and that the candidate is not an enrolled member of the Democratic Party. As such the assertion in the petition at paragraph 7, is false.

In response to the Objections, the Commissioners of the State Board of Election met on August 1, 2014, at which time they made the determination that 4,087 signatures were filed and, therefore, the petition did not contain the 15,000 signatures required to secure the designations in question. The Board also determined that Geeta Rankoth did not meet the age requirement to hold the office of New York State Comptroller. By a unanimous vote of the Board the petitions for all four candidates were held invalid. (See Determination dated August 1, 2014 attached hereto).

An objector is a necessary party to an action pursuant to Article 16 of the Election Law, and failure to name and serve an objector will result in dismissal. See Plochocki v. Onondaga County Board of Elections, 21 AD 3d 710 (4th Dept, 2005).

Here the Petitioners failed to name as a party and serve the Objectors. Accordingly, this action must be dismissed.

If you have any questions please do not hesitate to contact me.

Very truly yours,

Featherstonhaugh, Wiley & Clyne, LLP

Frank G. Hoare

FGH:

Attachments

{W0203801.1}

State of New York
STATE BOARD OF ELECTIONS

James A. Walsh
Chair
Douglas A. Kellner
Chair
Gregory P. Peterson
Commissioner
Andrew J. Spano
Commissioner

40 NORTH PEARL ST. STE5
ALBANY, N.Y. 12207-2729

Todd D. Valentine
Executive Director
Robert A. Brehm
Executive Director

August 1, 2014

STATE OF NEW YORK
STATE BOARD OF ELECTIONS

DETERMINATION

In the Matter of the objections of SCOTT K. BAILEY and VICTOR ANTONIO PEREZ to the Petition of the Democratic Party purporting to designate GEETA RANKOTH as a Candidate for the office of New York State Comptroller.

After an examination of the petition purporting to designate GEETA RANKOTH a candidate of the Democratic Party for the office of New York State Comptroller, and of the objections thereto, and the matter having been considered by the Commissioners of the State Board of Elections on August 1, 2014, it was determined that 4,087 signatures were filed, where 15,000 signatures are required to secure the designation in question. Further, specifications claim the designee does not meet the constitutional age requirement for the office being sought. Designee is 18 years of age, and the constitutional age requirement is 30. Therefore, the Board finds the petition is invalid.

Robert A. Brehm
Co-Executive Director

Todd D. Valentine
Co-Executive Director

FILED
NEW YORK STATE
BOARD OF ELECTIONS
ALBANY NEW YORK

2014 MAY 23 AM 9:18

State of New York)
ss.:
County of Suffolk)

KRISTEN STAVISKY, being duly sworn, says that she is the Assistant Secretary of the State Committee of the Democratic Party of the State of New York, and acted as such at the meeting duly convened and held at the Hilton Long Island, 598 Broad Hollow Road, Melville, New York, on May 21-22, 2014, and that the statements in the foregoing Certificate are true.

Kristen Stavisky

State of New York)
ss.:
County of Suffolk)

On the 22nd day of May in the year 2014 before me, the undersigned, personally appeared, KRISTEN STAVISKY personally known to me or proved to me on the basis of satisfactory evidence to be the individual whose name is subscribed to the within instrument and acknowledged to me that she executed the same in her capacity, and that by her signature on the instrument, the individual, or the person upon behalf of which the individual acted, executed the instrument.

JEANINE RENEE JOHNSON
Notary Public, State of New York
No. 02JO6291597
Qualified in New York County
Commission Expires Oct. 15, 2017

Notary Public

27

FILED
NEW YORK STATE
BOARD OF ELECTIONS
ALBANY NEW YORK

2014 MAY 23 AM 9: 17

State of New York)
ss.:
County of New York)

DAVID A. PATERSON, being duly sworn, says that he is the State Chair of the State Committee of the Democratic Party of the State of New York, and acted as such at the meeting duly convened and held at the Hilton Long Island, 598 Broad Hollow Road, Melville, New York, on May 21-22, 2014, and that the statements in the foregoing Certificate are true.

David A. Paterson

State of New York)
ss.:
County of New York)

On the 22nd day of May in the year 2014 before me, the undersigned, personally appeared, DAVID A. PATERSON personally known to me or proved to me on the basis of satisfactory evidence to be the individual whose name is subscribed to the within instrument and acknowledged to me that he executed the same in his capacity, and that by his signature on the instrument, the individual, or the person upon behalf of which the individual acted, executed the instrument.

05-22-2014

Notary Public

FILED
NEW YORK STATE
BOARD OF ELECTIONS
ALBANY, NEW YORK

2014 MAY 23 AM 9:17

CERTIFICATE OF DESIGNATION

The undersigned, David A. Paterson, State Chair and, Kristen Stavisky, Assistant Secretary of the State Committee of the Democratic Party of the State of New York ("State Committee") do hereby jointly and severally certify that, at a meeting of the State Committee duly convened and held at the Hilton Long Island. 598 Broad Hollow Road, Melville, New York, on May 21-22 2014, a quorum being present, a majority vote of the State Committee designated the following persons as candidates for the nominations of the Democratic Party of the State of New York for the statewide offices set forth opposite their names, such offices to be voted on at the Primary Election on September 9, 2014 and the November 4, 2014 General Election:

NAME OF CANDIDATE	RESIDENCE	OFFICE
Andrew M. Cuomo	4 Bittersweet Lane, Mt. Kisco, NY 10549	Governor
Kathy C. Hochul	405 Gull Landing Buffalo, New York 14202	Lieutenant Governor
Thomas P. DiNapoli	100 Great Neck Road, Great Neck Plaza, PO Great Neck, NY 11201	State Comptroller
Eric T. Schneiderman	645 West End Avenue Apt. 8F New York, NY 10025	Attorney General

We further certify that, at said meeting, the following persons were duly elected to serve as the committee to fill any vacancy in the foregoing designations:

Name:	Address:
Keith L.T. Wright	2225 Fifth Ave, Apt. ME New York, NY 10037
Sheila Comar	29 Depot Street, Middle Granville, NY 12849
Michael Reich	255 Breezy Way, Lawrence, NY 11559
Sherry Pavone	19 Fairwind Court, Northport, NY 11768

29

SUPREME COURT OF THE STATE OF NEW YORK
COUNTY OF ALBANY

In the Matter of the Application of Sam Sloan, as Candidate for Governor of the State of New York, Nenad Bach as Candidate for Lieutenant Governor of the State of New York, Geeta Rankoth as Candidate for Comptroller of the State of New York and Neil Grimaldi as Candidate for Attorney General of the State of New York

Petitioners-Candidates-Aggrieved

STATEMENT OF LAW

-against-

Index No. 4003-14

DOUGLAS A. KELLNER, ANDREW SPANO, JAMES A. WALSH and GREGORY P. PETERSON Commissioners and Constituting the NEW YORK STATE BOARD OF ELECTIONS

Respondents

ERIC T. SCHNEIDERMAN as Attorney General of the State of New York

---

For an Order Pursuant to Sections 16-100, 16-102 and 16-116 of the Election Law Declaring Valid the Designating Petitions purporting to Designate SAM SLOAN, NENAD BACH, GEETA RANKOTH and NEIL V. GRIMALDI as candidates for the Democratic Party nomination for Governor, Lieutenant Governor. Comptroller of New York State and attorney General of New York State respectfully at the Primary Election to be held at September 9, 2014 and restoring them to the Official Ballots of Such Primary Election

---

Neil Grimaldi, a New York attorney for the petitioner, states:

1) In **<u>Board of Estimate of City of New York v. Morris</u> 489 U.S. 688 (1988)** decided: March 22, 1989, the United States Supreme Court held as I am seeking which is the law of the United States. The United States Supreme Court held the Board of Estimates was illegally constituted because it violated

the Equal Protection Clause of the 14th Amendment to the constitution. So, the New York Board of Estimates was found to be null and void as a government agency, citing Reynolds vs. Sims, 377 US 533 and Abate vs Muss, 403 US 182. The Board of Elections completely denies voter equality by ignoring the voting rights of all voters, not Republican or Democrat. Also, Republican Voters have more voting power than Democrats because Democrats far exceed Republican voters. The NY Board of Elections and the New York City Board of Elections violate the Equal Protection Clause based on the disparity between Republicans and Democrats and the fact that so many millions of voters have no representative on the Board of Elections. This inequitable system at the board places the most prejudicial people as executives or board members by how they are chosen by representatives of the Democratic Party Chairperson and Republican Party Chairperson. Therefore, they cannot constitute a just body or forum to make legal and binding decisions.

This year at a recent July 2014 hearing of the New York City Board of Elections, Eliot Quinones was placed on the ballot by the clerk's report. Then without notice a new Board of Elections clerk's report put him off the ballot. These decisions excluded voters who properly signed the petition. New York Board of Elections clerk's report fundamentally put him off the ballot based on improper decisions excluding voters who properly signed the petition. The New York City Board of Elections also allows one representative and one representative for Brooklyn despite the fact that Brooklyn has three times as many voters as Richmond. This is exactly the reason why the Board of Estimates was found illegal by the United States Supreme Court. The Board of Elections in the City of New York is part of the New York State Board of Elections.

2) Reynolds vs Sims, 377 US 533 established that the Fourteenth Amendment of the United States Constitution established the principle of the equal protection clause and equal protection of the law. Required the Alabama legislature voting to be based on population. The Board of Elections ignores this landmark case and principle. This case stands for the fundamental principle of legislative government in the United States of equal representation for equal numbers of people. The right to vote is a personal right. The idea that one group can be granted greater voting strength as the board does excluding all Democratic and Republican voters than another is inconsistent with standards for popular representative government. Under the equal protection clause a claim of debasement of the right to vote through mal apportionment represents a practicable controversy. And the equal protection clause provides manageable standards for the lower courts to determine the constitutionality of a state legislative appointment scheme, citing Baker vs. Carr, 361 US 186. In addition it undercuts states

voters rights and the duly established United States Constitutional rights.

3) Oliver vs. Board of Education, 306 F. Supp. 1286, No. 69 Civ 2130, United States District Court for the Southern District of New York held that a statute creating the New York City School Board was unconstitutional where the statute provided that citizens of each borough elected one member of the school board. Statute diluted votes of the most populous boroughs. The way the New York State Board of Elections and New York City Board of Elections is organized violates the rights of all voters not Republican or Democratic and gives each Republican voter more power than each Democrat which is unequal and illegal. Also, voting procedures including proxy voting must follow one man one vote Atkins v. Monahan, 91 Misc. 2d 499, 399 NYS 2d 166.

4) Sergey v. King's County Republican Party, 459 F.2d 308 invalidated a county political party's rule on the voting procedure of the one party where each county committee member has an equal vote weighed according to the number of Republican voters in the district he represents. This violates the one-man one-vote principle established by the Supreme Court as a voters constitutional right. The amount of Democratic Party voters far exceeds the amount of Republican Party voters and gives one Republican and Democratic members equal power and not representing all other voters and Republican or Democratic violated the one-man one-vote constitutional law principle. The equal protection clause applies one man one vote even to count committeemen. Not giving a group the right to representation violates their constitutional rights and discriminates against them. See Moder v. Ogilive 394 US 814, 89 S.Ct. 1493

5) Fisher vs. Board of Supervisors, 59 Misc. 953; 301 NYS 2d 310 citing Seaman v. Fedourich, 16 NY 2d 94, 101 required the "one man one vote" principle required each votes be given equal weight. The Board of Elections excludes the rights of millions of voters and unfairly gives Republican voters more importance than an equal number of Democratic voters. See Burton vs. Schmidt, 128 Misc. 270.

6) The basic exclusion of the Board of Elections of the rights of millions of voters not Republican and Democrat is unequitably a violation of the equal protection clause of the Fourteenth Amendment see Reynolds vs. Sims, supra, Board of Estimates vs. Morris, supra.

7) The New York City Board of Elections has a long history of violating the United States voter's rights and insurgent Democratic and Republican voters rights including none of the other parties by the illegal

manner that members of the Board of Elections in New York City as elsewhere are chosen by the New York City Republican and Democratic Party political readers. This violates the Fourteenth Amendment due process requirements because the forum is not a just body and it is constituted in a way by giving undue and improper power to representatives of the Democratic and Republican Chairmen and their representatives who claim to me made a quasi-judicial body making legally binding decisions which they have harmful by their extensive officer and bureau members are selected illegally by the Political Democratic Party Chairmen and Republican Chairmen. It would be proper and legal only to have a civil service Board of Elections. The members of the Board of Electioms or an independent non-partisan non-prejudicial system of choosing Board of Election members statewide and in New York City and in each of our great New York County.

8) <u>The Respondents have refused to provide a legal basis in opposition to this motion because there is none.</u>

Whereas Petitioner is requesting an opportunity to subpoena witnesses and present evidence about the long history of political corruption caused by the illegal and improper manner the New York State Board of Elections and New York City Board of Elections are illegally formed, violative of the equal protection clause one man one vote and basic justice

DATED: August 8, 2014
Bronx, New York

Neil Grimaldi, Esq.
Attorney for Petitioners-Candidates
2860 Buhre Avenue, 1E
Bronx NY 10461

646-229-7974

SUPREME COURT OF THE STATE OF NEW YORK
COUNTY OF ALBANY

In the Matter of the Application of SAM SLOAN, as Candidate for Governor of the State of New York, NENAD BACH as Candidate for Lieutenant Governor of the State of New York, GEETA RANKOTH as Candidate for Comptroller of the State of New York and NEIL V. GRIMALDI as Candidate for Attorney General of te State of New York

Petitioners-Candidates-Aggrieved

-against-

DOUGLAS A. KELLNER, ANDREW SPANO, JAMES A. WALSH and GREGORY P. PETERSON Commissioners and Constituting the NEW YORK STATE BOARD OF ELECTIONS
Respondents

ERIC T. SCHNEIDERMAN as Attorney General of the State of New York

---

AFFIDAVIT AND MOTION TO TO SET ASIDE EVIDENCE SUBMITTED BY RESPONDENTS

Index No. 4003-14

For an Order Pursuant to Sections 16-100, 16-102 and 16-116 of the Election Law Declaring Valid the Designating Petitions purporting to Designate SAM SLOAN, NENAD BACH, GEETA RANKOTH and NEIL V. GRIMALDI as candidates for the Democratic Party nomination for Governor, Lieutenant Governor, Comptroller and Attorney General of New York State, respectfully at the Primary Election to be held at September 9, 2014 and restoring them to the Official Ballots of Such Primary Election

---

TO THE SUPREME COURT OF THE STATE OF NEW YORK:

COUNTY OF ALBANY

Neil Grimaldi, a New York Attorney for the petitioners, states the following:

1. The Evidence submitted by the respondent New York Board of Elections must be set aside by this Court because the Designating Petitions submitted by respondents were not original as required by New York State Laws of Evidence. The originals were 8.5 x 14 on green paper but the board submitted 8.5 x 11 copies, photo reduced.

2. The original petitions are in possession of the respondent and there was no basis for the original petitions not to be submitted, especially when the size and shape of the petitions are a major question of fact in this case.

3. The original petitions were on green color paper 8.5 x 14 and on card stock and not on these 8.5 x 11 reduced xeroxed photocopies which you can see are not originals.

4. The Court can clearly see that the designating petitions submitted by respondent are not original but are reduced copies.

5. Since the evidence submitted by respondents of the designating petitions have to be set aside, because they are not the original documents submitted by the petitioners, which original designating petitions are in the possession of the respondents at their office at 40 N. Pearl Street, which are only a few blocks from this court, there is no basis or reason the originals were not submitted as

required by law. The respondents have failed to submit adequate or sufficient evidence to undermine or invalidate the United States constitutional protected rights of the signers of these petitions and the rights of these candidates to be on the ballot. Judgment must be rendered for petitioners in this case so that the petition signers have a Constitutional protected right to have the candidates of their choice on the the ballot, which are SAM SLOAN, as Candidate for Governor of the State of New York, NENAD BACH as Candidate for Lieutenant Governor of the State of New York, GEETA RANKOTH as Candidate for Comptroller of the State of New York and NEIL V. GRIMALDI as candidate for Attorney General of New York. See Reynolds vs. Sims 377 US 533, Baker vs. Carr, 369 US 186 and Board of Estimate of City of New York v. Morris 489 U.S. 688 (1988).

6. The fact that the original petitions were 8.5 x 14 and on green paper and on card stock are not what respondents submitted which were 8.5 by 11 reduced photocopies, the acts of the respondents would appear to be fraudulent on the evidence they submitted especially considering the size of the petitions is such a crucial element of this case.

7. Sam Sloan, the petitioner, a very credible individual, testified that he was a math major at the University of California at Berkeley, is a book publisher and reprinter of more than 550 titles, and was the last non-lawyer ever to argue a case orally before the United

States Supreme Court, in a case that he won. SEC vs. Samuel H. Sloan, 436 US 103 (1978).

8. The unrefuted testimony of Sam Sloan as to how the proceedings at the Board of Elections took place clearly indicate that there were no witnesses or testimony regarding these candidates at the meeting of the Board of Elections on August 1, 2014 which would warrant them being placed off the ballot.

9. The only evidence was submitted by an attorney, Kimberly Galvin, and not by a witness.

10. Miss Galvin was not sworn in as a witness.

11. Miss Galvin did not testify in an adequate matter as to justify the boards actions.

12. Also, notice was required to the party who may be damaged by the actions of the Board.

13. The board acted based on Miss Galvin's statements. The board was as required by law to review the documents which was also a violation of the 14th Amendment due process clause which they did not do according to Sam Sloan's unrefuted testimony.

14. There were no Objections or Specifications as required by the New York Election Law Section 16-102 to the candidates at the board of election meeting against or in regard to Sam Sloan, Nenad Bach and Neil Grimaldi.

15. At the trial the only specifications entered into evidence concerned Geeta Rankoth. The evidence submitted to the board of elections at their hearing did not justify or substantiate their actions to invalidate any candidate on this slate.

16.Therefore there was insufficient evidence. This also shows that the board is a prejudiced body doing in the work of the Republican and Democratic State Chairman which is also a violation of the due process clause of the 14th Amendment. This is further reason why the board should be held unconstitutional because it is not a fair body or forum and does not properly represent all the voters of the state of New York. See Reynolds vs. Sims, supra and Baker vs. Carr, supra and Board of Estimate of City of New York v. Morris supra.

17. Miss Kimberly Galvin, an employee of Respondent Board of Elections, should have been called as a witness to refute the testimony of Sam Sloan. His unrefuted testimony clearly proves that the board acted unconstitutionally at its meeting on August 1, 2014 when these candidates were improperly and illegally put off the ballot. There is an inference that the court can draw against the

Board of Elections for their failure to call Miss Kimberly Galvin who was a witness to what happened at the Board of Elections meeting and her office is only a few blocks away. There are inferences to be drawn against the Board of Elections by their failure to produce the original designating petitions. At the hearing on August 11 there was a executive of the board of elections who could have been called to refute the testimony of Sam Sloan but was not called. There is an inference to be drawn from the failure to call this witness that Sam Sloan's testimony was truthful, which testimony was sufficient to invalidate the proceedings of the Board of Elections at their meeting on August 1 which invalidated these candidates without hearing any evidence or testimony against this slate of candidates, because there was no evidence or testimony to justify their actions. The Board of Elections failed to produce a brief or any case law to counter petitioners request to invalidate the Board of Elections. See Reynolds vs. Sims, supra and Baker vs. Carr, supra and Board of Estimate of City of New York v. Morris supra.

18. I move herein to add my name Neil Grimaldi as a petitioner and as a candidate for attorney general based on the fact that it was only a clerical mistake not to put me on as a petitioner in this case. Adding my name as petitioner in this case is consistent with my signing the motion as an attorney for the petitioners.

19. MY name as a petitioner is on the Statement of Law Submitted

heretofore.

20. The respondent is not prejudiced by my name being submitted as a candidate for Attorney General.

21. The meeting of the board of Elections on August 1, 2014 had no evidence submitted to invalidate me as an Attorney General candidate so therefore there is no basis to exclude me as an Attorney General candidate.

22. The petitioner signer's constitutional rights to have me as an attorney general candidate would be violated as the result of a clerical omission and that would be unconstitutional. Reynolds vs. Sims, supra and Baker vs. Carr, supra and Board of Estimate of City of New York v. Morris supra.

DATED: August 11, 2014
Bronx, New York

Neil Grimaldi

Neil Grimaldi, Esq.
Attorney for Petitioners-Candidates
2860 Buhre Avenue, 1E
Bronx NY 10461

646-229-7974

40

STATE OF NEW YORK
SUPREME COURT COUNTY OF ALBANY

In the Matter of the Application of Sam Sloan, as Candidate for Governor of the State of New York, Nenad Bach as Candidate for Lieutenant Governor of the State of New York, Geeta Rankoth as Candidate for Comptroller of the State of New York and Neil Grimaldi as Candidate for Attorney General of the State of New York,

Petitioners-Candidates-Aggrieved,

-against- Index No. 4003-14

DOUGLAS A. KELLNER, ANDREW SPANO, JAMES A. WALSH and GREGORY P. PETERSON Commissioners and Constituting the NEW YORK STATE BOARD OF ELECTIONS,

Respondents

ERIC T. SCHNEIDERMAN as Attorney General of the State of New York

---

For an Order Pursuant to Sections 16-100, 16-102 and 16-116 of the Election Law Declaring Valid the Designating Petitions purporting to Designate SAM SLOAN, NENAD BACH, GEETA RANKOTH and NEIL V. GRIMALDI as candidates for the Democratic Party nomination for Governor, Lieutenant Governor, Comptroller of New York State and Attorney General of New York State respectfully at the Primary election to be held at September 9, 2014 and restoring them to the Official Ballots of Such Primary Election

---

- E L E C T I O N P R O C E E D I N G S -

BEFORE: HON. ANDREW G. CERESIA,
Acting Justice of the Supreme Court

Transcript of the Proceedings held on the record on August 11, 2014, at the Albany County Courthouse, Albany, New York.

APPEARANCES:

NEIL GRIMALDI, ESQ.
2860 Buhre Avenue, Suite 1E
Bronx, New York 10461
Attorney for Petitioners-Candidates-Aggrieved

STATE OF NEW YORK STATE BOARD OF ELECTIONS
40 North Pearl Street, Suite 5
Albany, NY 12207-2729
By: KATHLEEN O'KEEFE, ESQ.
Attorneys for Respondent
New York State Board of Elections

THE COURT: The Court calls the case of the matter of Sam Sloan, et al, versus the Commissioners of the New York State Board of Elections, et al.

If I could ask counsel to state their appearances for the record at this time.

MR. GRIMALDI: I wouldn't go before distinguished counsel.

MS. O'KEEFE: Kathleen O'Keefe, counsel to the State Board of Elections.

MR. GRIMALDI: Neil Grimaldi. I gave her my address. 2860 Buhre Avenue, the Bronx. Thank you.

THE COURT: Okay. Mr. Grimaldi, whom do you have seated with you at counsel's table?

MR. GRIMALDI: This is the petitioner, Mr. Sam Sloan.

Please stand up, sir.

He's also the candidate for Governor. He's also the Petitioner. He signed the Verified Petition.

THE COURT: Okay. Thank you. The Court has reviewed all of the papers submitted on behalf of the Petitioners, as well as the papers submitted in opposition thereto.

The Court scheduled this matter for a hearing, however, in order to give each side, if they wish, the opportunity to be heard further in connection with their papers and/or present any evidence.

Certainly each party can rest on their papers if they would like, but with that said, Mr. Grimaldi, at this time do you wish to be heard any further and/or present any evidence to the Court in connection with this matter?

MR. GRIMALDI: Since I made such a long trip, I would like to say something short.

THE COURT: Sure.

MR. GRIMALDI: I cannot see any basis in law that the Board of Elections is in existence. It totally violates the United States Constitution. I have cited the case of Morris versus -- the Morris case, where the Board of Estimate was invalidated in New York City. Also invalidated the Board of Elections. So the Board of Elections no longer exist in New York.

I have a very deep love and affection for our democratic process. This process, one person, one vote, is very, very serious matter. At the New York City Board of Elections, which is part of this system, you know, it's a very, very corrupt system. It's an incredibly corrupt system unfortunately. I'm not saying the People are corrupt, but the system is corrupt, as indicated by the amount of cases that have to get reversed by the Court.

Now, I mentioned a case in my papers where I went to the Board of Elections, the man was valid on the ballot. He was Elliot Quinones. I mentioned his name. He was valid on the ballot and then they played a game on me. They went through petition signatures again. Somebody wanted to knock him off. So they knocked him off. Then I filed a motion, Order To Show Cause, and there were serious complications, but I had to go -- the new law of the Court of Appeals required me to go through every one of the petitions, signatures I was trying to get back.

And what they did was they invalidated him based on forgery. They had no right to do that. That has to be sent to the Court. They threw out signatures for an alteration. The alteration was just an alteration of the county. There wasn't, you know, an alteration has to be by a signature of the subscribing witness. There is a whole long process of cases that I represented. I represented insurgents in the Bronx and in Queens. And I constantly see that the Board is acting in an inappropriate manner. And that's totally an unfair system where the chairman of the political parties select the members of the Board. It's totally unconscionable. The most prejudice of people are on the Board.

Furthermore, in the Board of Estimate case, it's the same situation we have here with the New York City Board of Elections and the State Board of Elections. One man, one vote.

In the state there are so many more Democrats than Republicans. So the Republican has the same representation as the Democrat. That's totally unconscionable and in violation of the equal protection clause and one man one vote in the 14th Amendment.

In New York City the same thing exists, one man, one vote. One vote in Staten Island has the same equivalent of three to four Democrats in Brooklyn. The whole consciousness of this whole system is totally invalid. And then they bring forth -- these people then invite and bring in inspectors. Inspected by political clubs.

I ran for office of the District Attorney of the Bronx. I ran for various offices. I couldn't possibly confront the fraud that exists there. I once sectioned where I won the thing, but it was overturned. I couldn't afford. I'm a poor man, your Honor. I couldn't afford an inspector in every section. That would cost me in fifteen hundred people. I couldn't afford fifteen hundred people.

The law is very clear here, your Honor. And I have the greatest respect for counsel here and the other female counsel for the Board of Elections, but they didn't even respond, your Honor. There is no response to these papers. There is no case against that.

Furthermore, in this particular matter, as the papers clearly indicate, Mr. Sam Sloan, who is a publisher and very honorable gentleman, submitted signatures. There was no objections filed as required by Election Law and there was no specifications filed against his signatures.

He's entitled to due process of law of a notice. They didn't follow the law in throwing him off. They can't just throw you off unless they go through the proper procedures. This is a constitutionally invalid way of throwing him off.

On the second candidate. He has a candidate he put up unfortunately was too young, but there was no objections to her signatures.

I'm asking that your Honor throw her off, but the point that we get a chance to, through the vacancy committee, find another candidate.

I was a candidate for Attorney General. There was specifications filed against -- objections filed against me and specifications filed against me. I'm not saying there weren't in this particular situation.

So that situation -- the situation is different regarding the various candidates, your Honor. I'm not saying that they acted properly against me. All I'm saying is that which was filed against me in that form was a proper form. We had, as you know, your Honor, we had Mr. Cahill, who was a Republican, brought a case against to throw me off, but he withdrew the thing, as you know. So this is the only case pending.

We are asking that the voters get a chance to have a choice of candidates. That if I get thrown off as Attorney General, there is no choice for the Democratic Party. If Mr. Sloan gets thrown off, he gets denied his rights.

If the Comptroller candidate, this young lady gets thrown off, the Comptroller candidate for the Democratic Party has no choice for candidates.

The Federal Election Law -- I have had many Federal Election Law cases. The voters have the right to have their people heard and their candidates of their choice put up.

Mr. Sam Sloan is a very unique candidate. He has a very distinctive philosophy from many of the other candidates and I'm asking that he be given his opportunity, because the way they threw him off wasn't fair.

Your Honor, I also want to thank you very much for your graciousness, your Honor. I am very proud to be before you and I have had contacts with your staff and you have been most graciously kind in regard to this matter and I want to thank you most humbly for coming here and being here with us.

I'm not going to say it, but I'm very proud that I'm an Italian American, like you, your Honor. But I have to also say that I am so proud as America we have three of the most Irish judges here, like Judge Connolly. And I'm so proud to come to this Court and see such honorable, outstanding men who represent our government and justice fairly. And I thank you very much, your Honor, for the opportunity to be heard.

THE COURT: Okay. Thank you, Mr. Grimaldi.

Miss O'Keefe, do you wish at this time to be heard and/or present any evidence to the Court?

MS. O'KEEFE: Thank you, your Honor.

I do have a certified record of the petition in this case, a copy of the petition itself, as well as the general and specific objections that were filed.

There are a couple of things that I want to just bring, factual things I want to bring to the Court's attention.

THE COURT: Before you do that, would you like to offer those items into evidence?

MS. O'KEEFE: I would. I have it here. I have it separated out and I have a copy for Mr. Grimaldi.

THE COURT: If you could provide a copy to Mr. Grimaldi, and then we will have the other set marked for identification, please.

MS. O'KEEFE: As I said, this is the petition itself. You might want to have three exhibits. I don't know how you want to do this.

One is the general objection form for -- and it's specific for a Scott Bailey. And those are the objections against the petition for Geeta Rankoth. And that was the New York State Comptroller candidate.

And then we have the general and specific objections for Victor Perez. And these are objections also against Geeta Rankoth. So there was two objectors with respect to that candidate.

And then here is my certification on top.

THE COURT: Okay. And the petitions themselves are included there?

MS. O'KEEFE: This is the big stack, the petition right here.

THE COURT: Okay. We will have the petitions -- we will have each of the documents marked separately as you have identified them.

MS. O'KEEFE: So the record is clear, the petition has four volumes.

MR. GRIMALDI: Judge, I'm going to object.

THE COURT: Let me have them marked for identification and then I will give you a chance to be heard, okay?

MR. GRIMALDI: Of course, your Honor.

(Respondent's Exhibits 1 through 4 marked for identification.)

THE COURT: Mr. Grimaldi, the respondents have sought to introduce Exhibits 1 through 4. They have been identified for the record. Do you have any objection to the Court receiving those exhibits at this time?

MR. GRIMALDI: Yes, your Honor. Do you want me to stand?

THE COURT: You are fine.

MR. GRIMALDI: I have a little problem with my legs, your Honor.

THE COURT: You can remain seated.

What's your objection?

MR. GRIMALDI: One, my objections were the ones I set out in my motion, right, and my paperwork for constitutional basis.

One, that the Board of Elections improperly organized it. I don't think they have authority to do anything in regard to these. I think they are an invalid institution and they have no authority to do what, in fact, they did. One.

Two. There is no -- your Honor, I don't want to go any further without complimenting counsel. It's such a privilege how she presented this and the manner she did, but there is no objection against me here, your Honor. In the papers there is no specifications against me as required by the law of the State of New York.

There is objections here filed against Miss Geeta Rankoth, but there is no specifications against her. The law requires objections and specifications.

The other papers are that was objections by Victor Perez.

There is an objector Scott Bailey against the same individual, Geeta Rankoth, but there is no -- I have no specifications filed here.

So, therefore, I think that they are defective. And I also think, since there is no specifications or objections against my other candidate, including Mr. Sloan, the other candidate, Nenad Bach, I think that you have to leave them on.

THE COURT: Okay. I understand your objections. Those objections are overruled.

At this time the Respondent's 1 through and including 4 will be marked into the record at this time.

(Respondent's Exhibits 1 through 4 received in evidence.)

THE COURT: Ms. O'Keefe, you may continue at this time.

MS. O'KEEFE: Yes. I did move, in case the Court has only allowed them to be marked, I move them into evidence as a business record of the Board.

THE COURT: Okay. They have been received at this time.

MS. O'KEEFE: Thank you.

With respect to the facts Mr. Grimaldi has raised, I would like to clarify a few things for the Court.

As we have already mentioned with the Exhibit 2 and 3, there are general and specific objections against the candidate Geeta Rankoth. And it was in the letter that I sent to the Court, as well as to Mr. Grimaldi.

Those objections had basically alleged, and they are in the record, that she did not have the minimum number of signatures required, that she did not meet the age requirement for the office, and that she was not an enrolled member of the Democratic Party.

With respect to that particular candidate, the Board received time specific and general objections from two different objectors. And when the Board met on August 1st, the Board voted in public, and they are on a video that's available on YouTube, because they do have their meetings in public, with respect to that candidate, that she did not meet both the signature requirements, as well as the age requirement, and they held her Petition invalid. So that's a separate issue with regard to that candidate.

With respect to Mr. Grimaldi, Mr. Grimaldi's papers, his Order To Show Cause and his Petition to validate the Petition, does not ask for relief with respect to Mr. Grimaldi at all.

The application is only with respect to the three

other candidates. So there is no request before the Court whatsoever for affirmative relief with respect to Mr. Grimaldi's candidacy for Attorney General. So that's the other factual piece I wanted to bring to the Court's attention.

With respect to the other two candidates, that would be Mr. Sloan and that would be Nenad Bach. There were no general and specific objections filed with respect to those two candidates, however, in Election Law 6-154, the very first paragraph, and this is the section that deals with objections, and the objections are addressed in subdivision two.

But in subdivision one, and it's only one sentence, so I would like to read it to the Court.

Any petition filed with the officer or board charged with the duty of receiving it, shall be presumptively valid.

And this is the operative language.

If it is in the proper form and appears to bear the requisite number of signatures authenticated in the manner prescribed by the chapter.

So that's in the first subdivision of that section, because as an initial matter, the Board of Elections looks at the Petition to see is it in the proper form and appears to bear the requisite number of signatures. So the Board can do that on their own. It's a facial review of the Petition.

Subdivision two goes to objections that are thereafter filed.

Once the Petition has passed that first test, that facial test, it's presumptively valid, it passes the facial test, gets put in the valid category, and then unless objections come in, it's a valid petition.

In this instance, and the Court has the Petition before it, the Petition needed to contain 15,000 signatures.

Now, there are a number of infirmities in the Petition, but the most important issue here is that the Petition itself does not even contain 5,000 signatures. You don't have to look at individual signatures here. That is the total world of signatures.

So the Board didn't have to go through their records. They didn't have to identify a voter and then look and see how they registered, anything like that.

In order to be on the statewide ballot in a Designated Petition, you must have 15,000 signatures.

I had sent the Court my letter explaining the process that I just put on the record and pointing out that in all three determinations, two based on the objectors that filed objections, and the third based on that prima facie review that the Board is entitled to do pursuant to that section and subdivision, the Board of Elections determined that there were only 4,087 signatures in this Petition, far short of the 15,000.

So that's the facts of what the Board did.

There are a couple other quick pieces of information I need to bring to the Court's attention.

The State Board's configuration is found in the Constitution. That is Article two, Section eight of the New York State Constitution, which requires that the Board is made up of representatives from the two major parties.

As we know, there are other states where only one party controls the Board of Elections. In New York it's a bipartisan system. It's meant to be a check on each side. So I just wanted to bring that section to the Court's attention.

And then last. The Board, as I mentioned, does hold their meetings in public. If there is any question that the Board was doing a prima facie review, as I mentioned in 6-154, subdivision two, then the video actually shows the motion that was made at the time and that the Board was actually identifying that section was the basis of what their determination was made.

I do have something here. I will tell the Court if you are at all interested where to find that video. But I wanted to make that clear. I sent the Court the determination. Mr. Grimaldi has the same, but the video is available on YouTube and you can see the actual motion that's being made in the video.

THE COURT: Okay. Thank you, ma'am.

MR. GRIMALDI: May I retort briefly?

THE COURT: Go right ahead.

MR. GRIMALDI: First of all, your Honor, if they acted improperly in regard to those issues that I mentioned, then the fact is that my signature, my candidacy for Attorney General, should also be validated if that was done in a proper manner.

Two. The fact that it's in the Constitution of the State of New York doesn't mean that they can violate the United States Constitution, which is clearly separate.

I filed the notice here on the Attorney General to show that I'm filing objections to the way this is organized. And that provision in the Constitution is an illegal provision in the Constitution and it should be invalid.

I gave you the cases, the Morris case, which is totally definitive on this issue. The government cannot put up one case, not one piece of paper, not one case to retort definitively what I set forth.

Honestly, your Honor, I think you have no other choice but to hold the Board of Elections as an unconstitutional body as pursuant to the United States Constitution and the cases that I specified, equal protection, due process, and one man one vote.

Thank you very much, your Honor.

THE COURT: Thank you, sir.

MR. GRIMALDI: Mr. Sloan would like to speak. He's the petitioner. He has a right to speak if you don't mind, your Honor.

MR. SLOAN: These petitions were marked as valid. There is a website, Board of Elections website, and these petitions, all the candidates, Nenad Bach, Sam Sloan and Neil Grimaldi and Geeta Rankoth, those petitions were marked valid. They remained valid until August 4th, which was just a few days ago.

Suddenly on August 4th the website changed from valid to invalid. From the date these petitions were filed, up until August 4th, which was just one week ago, they were listed as valid. If they were going to mark them invalid, they should have notified us of these documents, this stack of papers they gave us right now. This is the first time we have seen these documents. We have never seen these documents before.

By the way, I never saw the Petition. The Petitions were collected by community organizers. They were the people who went around and say would you like to have this candidate. They go around and ask these different people. They go around collecting signatures, put them all together, they filed them with the Board of Elections.

So actually I have never seen in my life. I have never seen the Petitions in these. I saw them in a bundle. Physically I saw them, but I never had a chance to go through.

Suddenly they are bringing all these big stack of papers into the board room and they are saying the Court is supposed to rule on this, where we have not actually seen these documents before. Never saw them.

And then Mr. Grimaldi filed his Order to Show Cause a week ago. They have not responded to that. I haven't seen any response at all, any written responses. If there is, I haven't received it.

MR. GRIMALDI: Your Honor, may I call him as a

witness for a minute, two minutes? He was a witness. It'll be two minutes.

THE COURT: Sure. That's fine.

MR. GRIMALDI: Get up on the witness stand.

THE COURT: If you are going to give sworn testimony, you have to get sworn in first.

THEREUPON,

SAM SLOAN,

called as a witness, having been first duly sworn, was examined and testified as follows:

DIRECT EXAMINATION

BY MR. GRIMALDI:

Q Mr. Sloan, can you tell us your background in terms of education and profession?

A Oh yeah. I was a math major at the University of California Berkeley. I'm a publisher. I published over 550 books. Mostly I reprint old, out-of-print books. And I was a securities trader. I actually won a case against the Securities Exchange Commission in the United States Supreme Court, SEC against Samuel H. Sloan, 436 US 103 1978.

About six months ago there was a big article, nationwide article, about me on all the major newspapers because my case, which I argued orally pro se, was the last time any nonlawyer has ever been allowed to argue before the

United States Supreme Court. They made a rule pro se people cannot argue anymore. So that's why my picture was in the newspaper about six months ago. You can look it up. But the case is 1978. That's a long time ago.

But again, so I'm a book publisher. I have argued and won a case in the United States Supreme Court.

Q Can you tell us some classic books that you published?

MS. O'KEEFE: Your Honor, objection. This is completely irrelevant to the Election Law matter.

THE COURT: Sustained.

BY MR. GRIMALDI:

Q You were at the Board of Elections, their proceedings? Discuss what happened.

A I was at the meeting. It was not a hearing. It was a meeting on August 1st. And at that meeting a list of decisions had been made. It was a motion to make certain decisions about the Board. They read off the list of candidates and they were saying that these candidates we have determined they don't have enough signatures or for some reason there is an objection and we are removing those candidates.

And the Board voted on that and voted to remove those candidates. Then after that happened, Miss

Kimberly, a lawyer by the name of Kimberly, said we have some additional people we want to remove from the ballot. And then they read the names of the four candidates, myself and Nenad Bach and Geeta Rankoth and Neil Grimaldi.

And they said we want to add these people to the list of people we are throwing off the ballot and the Board said so moved and it passed.

I don't think the Board had ever seen these Petitions or these candidates listed. I personally have never seen the Petition. I did see them physically as a stack of papers, but as far as being able to look through them or leaf through them, this is the first time in my life I have ever seen them. They didn't serve these documents on us. We never had a chance to review them. I don't know where they got that count from, four thousand, five thousand votes, signatures. I don't know how many signatures are in there, because I didn't collect the signatures. Volunteers collected the signatures. Volunteers in the Bronx.

Q What kind of volunteers were they?

A Well, I will be perfectly frank with you. Many of the homeless shelters in the area, they give these ladies jobs, you know, give them some kind of work because they are homeless and they go around collecting signatures.

Q Now, let me ask you. Was there any evidence

presented at that hearing about regarding those petitions that you filed?

A No, none at all. There was not a single word was mentioned about the quality of the petitions, the number of petitions or anything. They just said -- Kimberly said, here is four more names we want to have people we want thrown off the ballot.

It was almost unbelievable, because the Board had just passed a motion with regard to specifications of objections. All these other people are thrown. They had objections filed against them.

These candidates did not have objections filed against them. So they are being thrown off without any general objections or specification objections and, of course, the specifications must be filed and general objections must be filed in three days. Specification must be filed in six days. No objections were filed in a timely basis against these candidates.

The one objection was against Geeta Rankoth. They mistakenly felt that she wasn't registered to vote. Actually, she had just become of legal age and she had just registered to vote. So they were mistaken about that too.

Q Looking at these petitions, prima facie, right, looking at those petitions, how many pages are there approximately?

A Roughly 4,000 pages there.

Q So prima facie, there could have been a sufficient amount of signatures to make up 15,000, right?

A Right. If all those signatures were good, there would be 15,000 signatures there.

Q There was no evidence filed at the hearing about the inadequacy at the hearing?

A There was no evidence, no even discussion. There was no discussion about the evidence, how many signatures there were. They didn't bring out the papers.

I have been to hearings before the Board of Elections and New York Board of Elections in the City of New York. And when somebody comes up --

MS. O'KEEFE: Your Honor, objection. The City of New York is not here before the Court.

THE COURT: Sustained.

A Okay. But, but, but anyway, these papers were not brought out. They were not shown to the Commissioners. The Commissioners didn't know that there was a big stack of papers or a small stack or two sheets of paper. They didn't know what they had.

So I don't think the Board actually knew what they were voting on.

And again, you can play this. I haven't seen it yet, but I'm sure it's on YouTube. It's going to come on YouTube. You can play the video over. And you can see what happens. You can see them voting to throw a bunch of candidates off the ballot. My candidates not included in the motion. And then suddenly at the end of the thing, they come back, oh yeah, we have four more candidates we want thrown off the ballot.

BY MR. GRIMALDI:

Q There was no evidence presented in that situation?

A No evidence of any kind.

Q And no petition?

A And no, they never saw the petition.

Q So the Board didn't see anything?

A Right.

Q Who testified? Miss Kimberly is a lawyer?

A Kimberly is a lawyer. She's the only one who spoke on this issue. No one else said anything.

MR. GRIMALDI: Thank you very much, your Honor.

THE COURT: Thank you.

Miss O'Keefe, any questions?

MS. O'KEEFE: Yes. Thank you, your Honor.

CROSS EXAMINATION

(Sam Sloan - Cross by Ms. O'Keefe)

BY MS. O'KEEFE:

Q Mr. Sloan, you have just testified that you have not seen that Petition previously; is that correct?

A I saw them physically as a stack of paper, but I did not collect the signatures. I did not assemble them. Other people in my neighborhood did.

Q And you have also just testified on the record under, you have been sworn, you have testified that you do not know how many signatures are in this Petition?

A That's right. I don't know.

Q And with respect to --

THE COURT: Excuse me one second.

MR. GRIMALDI: I'm sorry about the phone.

THE COURT: Let's get that shut off.

BY MS. O'KEEFE:

Q So with respect to the stack of papers that are there, the four volumes, you just testified there are 4,000 pages in that petition?

A I don't know. I don't know how many. I haven't counted the pages. I haven't had a chance. I just note it was listed as having 4,000 pages.

Q So you don't know if it's actually 4,000?

A No, I don't know.

Q Mr. Sloan, are you aware of how many sheets of

(Sam Sloan - Cross by Ms. O'Keefe)

paper are in a ream of paper? Are you aware of how many are in a ream? You buy paper, copy paper in reams?

A I suppose there is 500. I don't know.

Q That's right. And four thousand pages would be how many reams?

A I guess simple multiplication. It would be eight.

Q It would be eight. Does that stack of pages look like it's eight reams of paper?

A I'm not an expert on paper size.

MS. O'KEEFE: Your Honor, may I approach the witness?

THE COURT: You may.

MS. O'KEEFE: I would like to have Mr. Sloan look at the first volume of this petition.

THE WITNESS: Wait.

THE COURT: Hold on, sir. Let her -- let Miss O'Keefe ask a question. If your attorney has an objection, he may be heard on that.

BY MS. O'KEEFE:

Q Mr. Sloan, can you -- this is the first volume of the petition. Can you turn to page 14?

A Okay. This is page 14.

Q Page 14. Can you turn to the next page after page 14?

(Sam Sloan - Cross by Ms. O'Keefe)

A Eighteen.

Q So the page that followed page 14 is page 18?

A That's what it looks like.

Q Okay. Can you turn to the next page that follows 18?

A Okay.

Q What number is that?

A It says 22.

Q And can you turn to the next page after 22?

A Twenty-five.

Q Okay. So I don't want to take the Court's time and burden the Court with going through the entire Petition, but you have just testified that there are pages that are not sequential in this Petition; is that correct?

A Wait. Wait. The word sequential. I'm a mathematician by the way. I have a degree in mathematics from the University of California Berkeley.

Are you familiar with the Fibonacci series?

Q Mr. Sloan, I'm asking the questions, not you.

Is it true that the numbers in that Petition, that volume one, are not sequential?

You just testified it was 14, 18, 22, 25.

A Well, define sequential, because I have a different definition as a mathematician.

Q Are there gaps in the Petition pagination?

A According to what you just said there was one 14 and one was 18.

Q So would you agree there are gaps in the Petition's pagination?

A You are asking me to define the term of gaps and sequence. I just -- I just don't know. And I'm not sure what you are referring to actually.

MS. O'KEEFE: Thank you, Mr. Sloan. I will not burden the Court any further with this. It is in evidence. The Court can look at the Petition for itself.

BY MS. O'KEEFE:

Q With respect to the events that occurred at the meeting, would you agree or do you recollect that the Board of Elections commission has actually voted in several categories with respect to petitions?

MR. GRIMALDI: I object, your Honor. That's unclear. That's very broad, not clear.

MS. O'KEEFE: I will make that clearer.

THE COURT: Okay.

BY MS. O'KEEFE:

Q Mr. Sloan, did the Board vote in one category with respect to a facial review of the petitions?

A No, I'm sorry, I don't know the answer to that question.

Q Do you recall if the Board voted in a category with respect to specific objections that were filed against petitions?

A I'm sorry, I don't have a detailed recollection of these things. I mean, it's on the video someplace and we can play it, you know.

MS. O'KEEFE: I would like to get that exhibit from you and show you something else in the Petition.

Q This is volume four of the Petition.

A I would like to know why --

MR. GRIMALDI: Excuse me. Just answer the question, please.

BY MS. O'KEEFE:

Q Mr. Sloan, can you turn to the very last page of volume four? Can you tell the Court what the page number is at the bottom?

A 1402 it says.

Q And that is the last page of volume four; is that correct?

A Yes. It has no signature on it. So obviously there is something wrong there.

Q So you have testified that you believed there was

4,000 pages in this Petition, but that is the last page of the Petition, isn't it?

A It seems to be.

Q And that was, again, 1402?

A It says 1402.

MS. O'KEEFE: Thank you. I will take that exhibit back, Mr. Sloan.

BY MS. O'KEEFE:

Q Now, Mr. Sloan, you have said that you received no objections to your Petition; is that correct?

A That is correct.

Q Are you aware of any of the other candidates receiving copies of specific objections to their Petition?

MR. GRIMALDI: Objection. That's hearsay.

THE COURT: Overruled.

A Am I aware?

Q Are you aware of any specific objections being filed against any of the other three candidates?

A You just changed your question and asked a different question.

Q No. I said are you aware of any specific objections being filed against the other three candidates?

A No.

Q You are not aware of that. Okay.

MS. O'KEEFE: Thank you, your Honor. I have no further questions.

MR. GRIMALDI: I'm finished, your Honor. Thank you very much.

THE COURT: Sir, you may step down. Thank you.

Mr. Grimaldi, for the purpose of this hearing, do you rest at this time?

MR. GRIMALDI: Yes.

THE COURT: Miss O'Keefe, for the purpose of this hearing, do you rest at this time?

MS. O'KEEFE: Yes, I do, your Honor, with one caveat. I just want to direct the Court's attention to 6-154, subdivision one in the Election Law, which authorizes the prima facie review.

THE COURT: All right. I want to thank all counsel for your time today. The Court will, again, has already reviewed the papers evidence submitted. The Court will take into account everything that was set forth today on the record, along with the evidence that has been submitted here in this hearing. The Court will reserve at this time and issue a written decision and order. Thank you all for your time.

MS. O'KEEFE: Thank you, your Honor.

MR. GRIMALDI: Thank you very much, your Honor.

It's a real privilege to be here before you, your Honor. Send my regards to your clerk. Thank you very much.

THE COURT: Thank you, Mr. Grimaldi.

Thank you, Miss O'Keefe.

(Whereupon the proceedings were concluded.)

* * *

I N D E X

PETITIONER'S WITNESSES

NAME	DIRECT	CROSS	REDIRECT	RECROSS
Sam Sloan	21	26	--	--

RESPONDENT'S EXHIBITS

NO.	DESCRIPTION	IDENT.	EVID.
1	Certification from Board of Elections	11	13
2	Objections of Victor Perez (general & specific) re Petition of Geeta Rankoth	11	13
3	Objections of Scott Bailey (general & specific) re petition of Geeta Rankoth	11	13
4	Four volumes of the Petition at issue	11	13

C E R T I F I C A T I O N

I, Tracie Pamela Hilton, C.S.R, R.P.R., a Senior Court Reporter for the Unified Court System, Third Judicial District of the State of New York, do hereby certify that I attended and reported the foregoing proceedings; that it is a true and accurate transcript of the proceedings had therein to the best of my knowledge and ability.

Tracie Pamela Hilton
Certified Shorthand Reporter
Registered Professional Reporter

Dated: August 14, 2014

UNITED STATES DISTRICT COURT
NORTHERN DISTRICT OF NEW YORK

SAM SLOAN; NEIL V. GRIMALDI; NEREIDA NARVEAZ; VENIADA QUINONES; MILLIE QUINONES; TIARA LAWRENCE; and TRINA JACKSON,

Plaintiffs,

vs.

1:14-cv-01071 (MAD/CFH)

NEW YORK STATE BOARD OF ELECTIONS, Commissioners Douglas A. Kellner, Andrew Spano, James A. Walsh, Gregory P. Peterson; ERIC T. SCHNEIDERMAN, as Attorney General of the State of New York,

Defendants.

APPEARANCES: **OF COUNSEL:**

SAM SLOAN
2860 Buhre Avenue
Suite 1E
New York, New York 10461
Plaintiff *pro se*

NEIL V. GRIMALDI
2860 Buhre Avenue
Suite 1E
New York, New York 10461
Plaintiff *pro se*

NEREIDA NAREAZ
1815 Davidson
Bronx, New York 10453
Plaintiff *pro se*

VENIADA QUINONES
1815 Davidson
Bronx, New York 10453
Plaintiff *pro se*

MILLIE QUINONES
1921 Jerome Avenue
Bronx, New York 10453
Plaintiff *pro se*

TIARA LAWRENCE
1921 Jerome Avenue
Bronx, New York 10453
Plaintiff *pro se*

TRINA JACKSON

NEW YORK BOARD OF ELECTIONS
40 North Pearl Street
Suite 5
Albany, New York 12207

OFFICE OF THE NEW YORK STATE ATTORNEY GENERAL
Albany Office
The Capitol
Albany, New York 12224

Mae A. D'Agostino, U.S. District Judge:

ORDER TO SHOW CAUSE

The Court has considered Plaintiffs' complaint, the motion for order to show cause and the exhibits attached thereto. On the basis of these papers, Plaintiffs have sufficiently shown good and sufficient cause why the standard Notice of Motion procedure cannot be used and that the Court should dispense with the Notice of Motion requirement of Local Rule 7.1(b).

Based on the foregoing, the Court hereby

ORDERS that Defendants show cause, if there be any, to this Court by submission on papers as ordered herein, before the Honorable Mae A. D'Agostino, United States District Court Judge at the United States Courthouse, 445 Broadway, Albany, New York, why an order should not be made and entered herein restoring Sam Sloan on the ballot as a candidate for Governor of New York State, Nenad Bach as a candidate for Lieutenant Governor of New York State, Geeta

Rankoth as a candidate for Comptroller of New York State, and Neil V. Grimaldi as a candidate for Attorney General of New York State, in the Democratic Primary to be held on September 9, 2014; and the Court further

ORDERS that Plaintiffs shall serve a copy of this Order to Show Cause together with a copy of the papers upon which it is based, by delivery to the New York State Board of Elections at 40 N. Pearl Street, Albany, New York 12207 and upon the Attorney General of the State of New York at the Robert Abrams Building, Albany, New York, on or before **1:00 p.m. on September 3, 2014** and upon the other Defendants by certified mail; and the Court further

ORDERS that Defendants shall serve and file any opposition to Plaintiffs' motion on or before **September 5, 2014 at 1:00 p.m.**; and the Court further

ORDERS that Plaintiffs shall serve and file any reply papers on or before **September 5, 2014 at 5:00 p.m.**; and the Court further

ORDERS that no personal appearance is required – the papers will be taken on submission – unless otherwise directed by the Court.[1]

IT IS SO ORDERED.

Dated: September 2, 2014
Albany, New York

Mae A. D'Agostino
U.S. District Judge

---

[1] The Court notes that Plaintiffs' motion for an order to show cause failed to strictly comply with Local Rule 7.1. The Court also has concerns regarding the merits of Plaintiffs' complaint which, upon brief inspection, largely appears to be subject to dismissal for several reasons. *See, e.g., Fischer v. Suffolk County Bd. of Elections*, No. 08-cv-4171, 2009 WL 2524859 (E.D.N.Y. Aug. 14, 2009). In light of the time sensitive nature of this matter, however, the Court has directed a response by Defendants.

UNITED STATES DISTRICT COURT
NORTHERN DISTRICT OF NEW YORK

--X

SAM SLOAN, NENAD BACH, GEETA RANKOTH, NEIL V. GRIMALDI, MILLIE QUINONES, TRINA JACKSON, TIARA LAWRENCE, NEREIDA NARVEAZ, and VENIADA QUINONES,

Plaintiffs,

-against-

NEW YORK STATE BOARD OF ELECTIONS, Commissioners Douglas A. Kellner, Andrew J. Spano James A. Walsh, Gregory P. Peterson, ERIC T. SCHNEIDERMAN, as Attorney General of the State of New York,

Defendants.

--X

AFFIRMATION IN OPPOSITION
1:14-cv-01071
(MAD/CFH)

KATHLEEN O'KEEFE, an attorney-at-law duly admitted to the practice of law before the United States District Court, Northern District of New York and not a party to the above captioned matter, affirms the following to be true under the penalties of perjury pursuant to CPLR 2106:

1. I am Co-Counsel to the New York State Board of Elections and attorney for respondents James A. Walsh, Douglas A. Kellner, Andrew J. Spano and Gregory P. Peterson in their official capacities as Commissioners of the State Board of Elections, and the New York State Board of Elections, above-captioned proceeding.

2. I am personally and fully familiar with all the facts and circumstances herein and submit this affirmation in opposition to the relief sought in the Complaint for the reasons set forth herein and in Defendents' Memorandum of Law.

STATEMENT OF FACTS

3. The State Board of Elections received a designating petition purporting to designate Sam Sloan a candidate of the Democratic Party for the office of Governor of the State of New York, Nenad Bach a candidate of the Democratic Party for the office of Lt. Governor of the State of New York, Neil V. Grimaldi a candidate of the Democratic Party for the office of New York State Attorney General and Geeta Rankoth a candidate of the Democratic Party for the office of New York State Comptroller.

4. Subsequently, General Objections and Specifications of Objections were filed by three different objectors with respect to the petition for Neil V. Grimaldi.

5. One objector stated that the candidate claimed 5,113 signatures and that the actual number of valid signatures was zero.

6. The second objector claimed that the petition contains 4,476 signatures, far short of the 15,000 needed.

7. The third objector claimed that the petition does not contain the minimum number of signatures required and fails to contain signatures from one half of the congressional districts in the state as required.

8. In addition, General Objections and Specifications of Objections were filed by two objectors with respect to the petition for Geeta Rankoth.

9. Both objectors claimed that the petition fails to contain the minimum number of signatures required, that the candidate does not meet the age requirement to hold the office, and that the candidate is not an enrolled member of the Democratic Party.

10. The Commissioners of the State Board of Elections met on August 1, 2014, at which time they made the determination that 4,087 signatures were filed and, therefore, the petition did not contain the 15,000 signatures required to secure the designations in question.

11. The Board also determined that Geeta Rankoth did not meet the age requirement to hold the office of New York State Comptroller.

12. By a unanimous vote of the Board the petitions for all four candidates were held invalid.

13. A special proceeding was thereafter commenced by attorney/candidate Neil Grimaldi in the New York State Supreme Court to validate the petition with respect to Sam Sloan, Nenad Bach and Geeta Rankoth and to substitute another person for Geeta Rankoth.

14. The relief requested did not include an application to validate the petition with respect to Neil Grimaldi.

15. The Supreme Court held a hearing on Monday, August 11, 2014.

16. Subsequently, attorney/candidate Grimaldi sought to add himself as party and the Supreme Court rejected his untimely request after the hearing had concluded.

17. By Decision/Judgment/Order dated August 12, 2014 (Ceresia, J.) denied the relief requested (Exhibit 1).

18. Thereafter, Plaintiffs appealed to the New York Supreme Court, Appellate Division, Third Department.

19. That Court affirmed the Supreme Court Decision/Order/Judgment in a unanimous decision (Exhibit 2).

20. In doing so, the Appellate Division cited New York State Court of Appeals' precedents when addressing the plaintiffs' failure to name and serve individuals who objected to the Rankoth petition (*see Matter of Gadsen v Board of Elections of City of N.Y.*, 57 NY2d 751, 752 [1982]; *Matter of Biscone v Scaringe*, 59 NY2d 794 [1982]) and held that such failure constitutes a jurisdictional defect.

21. This is settled New York law.

22. The Appellate Division also rejected plaintiffs' argument that the State Board of Elections' composition is unconstitutional because it violates the Equal Protection Clause's requirement of "one person, one vote." The Court relied on federal precedents, from both the United States Supreme Court (*Hadley v Junior College Dist. of Metropolitan Kansas City*, 397 US 50, 54 [1970]; *Sailors v Board of Educ. of County of Kent*, 387 US 105, 111 [1967]) and the Second Circuit Court of Appeals (*Rosenthal v Board of Educ. of Cent. School Dist. No. 3 of Town of Hempstead,* 497 F2d 726, 729 [2d Cir 1974]), which held that the one person one vote principle does not apply to an appointive board charged with administrative duties.

23. This is settled Federal law.

24. Finally, the Appellate Division affirmed Supreme Court's holding that the State Board of Elections was free to perform a facial review of the petitions to determine if they are "in proper form and appear to bear the requisite number of signatures," relying on Election Law § 6-154(1), and concluded that the petitions were invalid for lack of sufficient signatures.

25. Thereafter, plaintiffs sought leave to appeal in the New York State Court of Appeals.

26. Oral argument was heard on the matter and the Court of Appeals denied leave (Exhibit 3).

THE APPLICATION FOR AN INJUNCTION SHOULD BE DENIED AND THE COMPLAINT SHOULD BE DISMISSED

27. Plaintiffs seek the same relief in this matter, concerning the same candidates and designating petition, that was sought in the New York Courts.

28. In seeking such relief, plaintiffs make the same arguments already made in the New York proceeding and are challenging the results of that proceeding.

29. Based on the foregoing, and the legal arguments set forth in Defendants' Memorandum of Law, this Court should deny the request for an injunction and dismiss the Complaint.

Dated: September 5, 2014
Albany, New York

Kathleen O'Keefe

Kathleen O'Keefe, Esq.
Co-Counsel
New York State Board of Elections
40 North Pearl St., Suite 5
Albany, NY 12207-2729
kathleen.okeefe@elections.ny.gov
T (518) 474-2063
F (518) 486-6627

UNITED STATES DISTRICT COURT
NORTHERN DISTRICT OF NEW YORK
---X

SAM SLOAN, NENAD BACH, GEETA RANKOTH, NEIL V. GRIMALDI, MILLIE QUINONES, TRINA JACKSON, TIARA LAWRENCE, NEREIDA NARVEAZ, and VENIADA QUINONES,

Plaintiffs,

-against-

NEW YORK STATE BOARD OF ELECTIONS, Commissioners Douglas A. Kellner, Andrew J. Spano James A. Walsh, Gregory P. Peterson, ERIC T. SCHNEIDERMAN, as Attorney General of the State of New York,

Defendants.
---X

MEMORANDUM OF LAW
1:14-cv-01071
(MAD/CFH)

Plaintiffs' suit is barred by the *Rooker–Feldman* doctrine whereby "federal district courts lack subject matter jurisdiction over suits that are, in substance, appeals from state-court judgments" *Fisher v. Suffolk County Bd.of Elections*, 2009 WL 2524859, 3 (citing *Rooker v. Fidelity Trust Co.*, 263 U.S. 413, 414-415 [1923]). This matter meets the four requirements for the application of the doctrine:

> (1) the federal-court Plaintiff must have lost in state court; (2) the Plaintiff's injuries must be caused by the state court judgment; (3) the Plaintiff's claims must invite the district court to review and reject that state court judgment; and (4) the state-court judgment must have been rendered prior to the commencement of the district court proceedings

Id. (citing *Hoblock v. Albany County Bd. Of Elections*, 422 F.3d 77, 85 [2d Cir. 2005]).

Plaintiffs make the same claims as they made in the New York Courts about the same candidates and the same designating petition. Plaintiff are seeking to challenge the results of the New York matter and the *Rooker–Feldman* doctrine applies.

Plaintiffs' claim is also barred by the doctrine of issue preclusion. *Wolff v. City of N.Y. Fin. Servs. Agency*, 939 F. Supp. 258, 264-265 (S.D.N.Y. 1996) (citing *Migra v. Warren City Sch. Dist.*, 465 U.S. 75, 83 (1984). Plaintiffs made their claim in the New York Courts based on the same grounds stated herein and had a full opportunity to be heard on those claims. Their motion for an injunction should be denied and the complaint dismissed.

Kathleen O'Keefe, Esq.
Co-Counsel
New York State Board of Elections
40 North Pearl St., Suite 5
Albany, NY 12207-2729
kathleen.okeefe@elections.ny.gov
T (518) 474-2063
F (518) 486-6627

STATE OF NEW YORK
SUPREME COURT COUNTY OF ALBANY

In the Matter of the Application of
SAM SLOAN, as Candidate for Governor of the State of New York, NENAD BACH, as Candidate for Lieutenant Governor of the State of New York, and GEETA RANKOTH, as Candidate for Comptroller of the State of New York,

Petitioners,

-against-

DECISION/ORDER/ JUDGMENT

DOUGLAS A. KELLNER, ANDREW SPANO, JAMES A. WALSH, and GREGORY P. PETERSON, Commissioners and Constituting the NEW YORK STATE BOARD OF ELECTIONS, and ERIC T. SCHNEIDERMAN, Attorney General of the State of New York,

Respondents.

All Purpose Term
Hon. Andrew G. Ceresia, Acting Supreme Court Justice
Index No. 4003-14

Appearances:[1]

Neil Grimaldi, Esq.
Attorney for Petitioners
2860 Buhre Avenue
Bronx, New York 10461

Kathleen O'Keefe, Esq.
For Respondent New York State
Board of Elections
40 North Pearl Street
Albany, New York 12207-2108

1 Although the Attorney General was a named respondent and was served with the petition, that office advised the Court that it would not be participating in this matter.

Ceresia, J.

Petitioners, arguing that respondent New York State Board of Elections (hereinafter "the Board") improperly invalidated their designating petitions as Democratic Party candidates for statewide offices, commenced the above-captioned proceeding pursuant to Election Law § 16-100 *et seq.* to validate their designating petitions. Petitioners also seek to have the Board declared null and void as violative of the federal constitution and federal law. Finally, petitioners seek attorney's fees. The Board opposed, asserting that petitioners' designating petitions were invalidated because they contained fewer than the minimum number of required signatures, and because petitioner Geeta Rankoth was found not to be of the minimum age required to hold the office of Comptroller.

The Court held a hearing on August 11, 2014, for the purpose of allowing the parties to be heard further and/or present evidence. Petitioners elicited sworn testimony from petitioner Sam Sloan, without objection from the Board. The Board offered into evidence copies of two sets of general and specific objections by Victor Perez and Scott Bailey (Exhibits 2 and 3, respectively), copies of petitioners' designating petitions (Exhibit 4), and a certification indicating that the aforementioned documents were true and exact copies of the originals (Exhibit 1). Petitioners asserted specific objections to the admission of these documents, arguing that the documents should not come into evidence because the Board is unconstitutionally organized and was without authority to act in the absence of objections. Petitioners, however, did not raise any foundational objections or any other objections impacting the admissibility of the documents. As such, the Court overruled petitioners' objections – which, again, bore no relevance to the actual admissibility of the documents in question – and received the exhibits into evidence.[2]

Turning first to the candidacy of Grimaldi – petitioners' counsel, who seeks to run for the office of New York State Attorney General – it is noted that Grimaldi was not named as a party in the petition commencing this proceeding. Rather, in the same affidavit/motion which set forth petitioners' best evidence objection, petitioners also for the first time seek to add Grimaldi as a named petitioner. Noting that the return date in this matter has passed and the hearing has already been concluded, this application is denied as untimely. In any event, even if Grimaldi were to be added as a named petitioner, he still would not be entitled to the relief that he seeks, for the same reasons set forth below with respect to petitioners Sam Sloan and Nenad Bach.

2

On August 12, 2014, the day after the hearing was concluded, petitioners faxed to the Court an unsworn affidavit/motion from Neil Grimaldi, Esq. No indication has been provided to the Court that said affidavit/motion was served on respondents. Pursuant to the affidavit/motion, petitioners argue for the first time that the best evidence rule prohibited admission into evidence of copies of the designating petitions (Exhibit 4). This objection is untimely. In that regard, the Court notes that, had that objection been raised in a timely manner during the hearing as it was required to be, the Board would have had the chance to be heard on the matter, the Court would have had the opportunity to make a ruling, and the Board ultimately would have had the chance to cure the defect, if any. Accordingly, the petitioners' untimely best evidence objection is now overruled.

Next, with respect to the candidacy of Geeta Rankoth, the instant petition is jurisdictionally defective because, although objections were filed to Rankoth's designating petitions, Rankoth failed to name and serve the objectors, who are necessary parties to a proceeding to validate designating petitions (see Matter of Gadsen v Bd. of Elec. of City of N.Y., 57 NY2d 751, 752 [1982]; Matter of Plochocki v Onondaga County Board of Elections, 21 AD3d 710, 710 [2005]; Matter of Fusco v Westchester County Bd. of Elec., 286 AD2d 456, 456-457 [2001], lv denied 96 NY2d 718 [2001]). Nevertheless, even considering the merits of the petition as it relates to Rankoth, the Board properly ruled that Rankoth's designating petitions were invalid because Rankoth did not meet the age requirement to hold the office of New York State Comptroller, and because her designating petitions contained fewer than the minimum number of signatures. Petitioners concede that Rankoth is too young for the position, and the record reveals that Rankoth's designating petitions contained only 4,087 signatures, far short of the necessary 15,000 (see Election Law § 6-136 [1]). Therefore, the instant petition is denied as it pertains to Rankoth.

With regard to petitioners' further argument that Rankoth should be replaced by a committee on vacancies rather than having her petitions invalidated, "a designated committee to fill vacancies may act only if the designating petition itself is deemed valid" (Matter of Elgin v Smith, 10 AD3d 483, 484 [2004]; see Matter of Owens v Sharpton, 45 NY2d 794, 795 [1978]; Matter of Marcatante v Lundy, 8 Misc 2d 313, 316-317 [1957], affd 4 AD2d 883 [1957]). Here, since Rankoth's designating petitions were invalid, the committee on vacancies is not empowered to name a replacement candidate.

Turning to the candidacies of Sloan and Bach, petitioners claim that the Board acted beyond the scope of its authority and in an arbitrary and capricious manner by invalidating their designating petitions without any objections having been filed. However, under Election Law § 6-154 (1), the Board has the authority to perform a ministerial, facial review of designating petitions to determine whether they are in the proper form and appear to bear the requisite number of signatures (see Matter of Rosen v McNab, 25 NY2d 798, 799 [1969]; Matter of Mansfield v Epstein, 5 NY2d 70, 73 [1958]). The Board may make such a determination even in the absence of objections (see Casler v Bd. of Elec. of Herkimer County, 131 Misc 744, 746 [1928]; see also Jerry H. Goldfeder, Goldfeder's Modern Election Law § 4 [C], at 37; 50 NY Jur 2d Elections § 371). Here, the Board acted properly in conducting a facial review of the designating petitions and then invalidating said petitions on the basis that they did not contain the requisite number of signatures. In that regard, it is noted that even the most cursory facial review of the designating petitions clearly reveals that they could not possibly contain the necessary 15,000 signatures. That is, the last numbered page of the submitted designating petitions was 1,402, and each page allotted for no more than 10 signatures. Thus, even 1,402 pages with 10 signatures on each page would fall approximately 1,000 signatures short of what was needed. Further, there are numerous and significant gaps in pagination such that it is clear that there were significantly fewer than 1,402 pages of designating petitions filed. In addition to that, numerous pages contain fewer than the full allotment of 10 signatures. Therefore, it is clear that the Board acted well within the scope of its authority, was not arbitrary or capricious, and properly invalidated the designating petitions for lack of signatures, even in the absence of objections. Accordingly, the instant petition is denied with respect to Sloan and Bach.

As a final matter, petitioners argue that the composition of the Board violates the federal constitution and federal law because it is made up only of Democrats and Republicans, with no representation by independent voters or minor party members, and thus violates the "one man, one vote" principle. However, "[s]ince the choice of members of the [Board] did not involve an election and since none was required for these nonlegislative offices, the principle of 'one man, one vote' has no relevancy" (Sailors v Bd. of Ed. of Kent County, 387 US 105, 111 [1967]; see Cohanim v New York City Bd. of Ed., 204 F Supp 2d 452, 453 [2002] [holding that the "one person, one vote" standard does not apply to appointed bodies]). As such, petitioners' claim in this regard is without merit.

Accordingly, it is hereby

ORDERED AND ADJUDGED that the petition is denied.

This shall constitute the decision and order of the Court. The original decision and order is returned to the attorney for BOE. All other papers are being delivered to the Supreme Court Clerk for delivery to the County Clerk or directly to the County Clerk for filing. The signing of this decision and order and delivery of this decision and order does not constitute entry or filing under CPLR Rule 2220. Counsel is not relieved from the applicable provisions of that rule respecting filing, entry and notice of entry.

DATED: August 12, 2014
Troy, New York

Andrew G. Ceresia
Acting Supreme Court Justice

Papers Considered:
1. Verified Petition dated August 4, 2014;
2. Letter of Helena Lynch, Esq., dated August 6, 2014;
3. Letter of Kathleen O'Keefe, Esq., dated August 7, 2014, and Exhibits;
4. Letter of Frank G. Hoare, Esq., dated August 7, 2014, and Exhibits.
5. Statement of Law of Neil Grimaldi, Esq., dated August 8, 2014;
6. Affidavit/Motion of Neil Grimaldi, Esq., dated August 11, 2014, received August 12, 2014.

State of New York
Court of Appeals

Decided and Entered on the
twenty-seventh day of August, 2014

Present, HON. JONATHAN LIPPMAN, *Chief Judge, presiding.*

Mo. No. 2014-926
In the Matter of Sam Sloan, &c.,
et al.,
Appellants,
v.
Douglas A. Kellner et al., &c.,
Respondents,
et al.,
Respondent.

Appellants having moved for leave to appeal to the Court of Appeals in the above cause;

Upon the papers filed and due deliberation, it is

ORDERED, that the motion is denied.

Andrew W. Klein
Clerk of the Court

State of New York
Court of Appeals

Andrew W. Klein
Chief Clerk and
Legal Counsel to the Court

Clerk's Office
20 Eagle Street
Albany, New York 12207-1095

Decided August 27, 2014

Mo. No. 2014-926

In the Matter of Sam Sloan, &c., et al.,
Appellants,
v.
Douglas A. Kellner et al., &c.,
Respondents,
et al.,
Respondent.

Motion for leave to appeal denied.

UNITED STATES DISTRICT COURT
NORTHERN DISTRICT OF NEW YORK

Sam Sloan, Nenad Bach, Geeta Rankoth, Neil V. Grimaldi, Millie Quinones, Trina Jackson, Tiara Lawrence, Nereida Narveaz and Veniada Quinones,

14 CV 1071

Plaintiffs

REPLY TO AFFIRMATION IN OPPOSITION

-against-

Douglas A. Kellner, Andrew Spano, James A. Walsh, Gregory P. Peterson, Commissioners and Constituting the New York State Board of Elections, Eric T. Schneiderman as Attorney General of the State of New York, Kimberley Galvin, Kathleen O'Keefe, Brian D. Rusk, Hilda B. Classon, Marc A. Landis, Jeremy D. Richardson, Scott K. Bailey and Victor Antonio Perez,

Defendants

Neil Grimaldi, petitioner, an attorney (although not a member of the bar of the Northern District of New York) states the following in reply to the Affirmation of Kathleen O'Keefe:

1. This case is different than the case in the New York State Supreme Court and Appellate Division and the cases referred to by Miss O'Keefe because this case involves the basic constitutional rights of Sam Sloan and Nenad Bach.

2. This case involves the rights of five voters, unlike the case in New York Supreme Court. These five voters were not part of the state board's case and they have separate constitutional rights to have the candidates of their choice on the ballot and the prior case cannot preclude their rights. See Baker vs. Carr, 361 US 186, Reynolds vs. Sims, 377 US 533.

3. This case is different than the cases cited by Miss O'Keefe because in this case the basic constitutional rights of Sam Sloan and and Nenad Bach were violated in that there were no objections of specifications filed against them. They did not receive their rights under the 14th amendment to notice and a hearing before their United States Constitutional rights were removed from them.

4. Miss O'Keefe has failed to mention that there was never any evidence of specifications or objections filed against Sam Sloan or Nenad Bach.

5. The specifications and arguments about insufficient age filed against Geeta Rankoth are not objections to the candidacy of Sam Sloan and Nenad Bach as there were no objections filed against them as to the insufficiency of their age or candidacy.

6. The case mention of Fischer v. Suffolk County Bd. of Elections, No. 08-cv-4171, 2009 WL 2524859 (E.D.N.Y. Aug. 14, 2009) does not apply to this case because in that case there was no claim of constitutional rights violated. That case only had to do with the inadequate amount of signatures.

7. Petitioners are acting pro se without counsel and therefor technical and not substantial procedural matters should be waived and ignored.

8. The cover sheets claimed that the candidates had a sufficient amount of signatures and thus there was no basis to invalidate them without a hearing.

9. There was no prior request of this applications by the petitioner voters and their rights should not be violated.

10. The New York State Supreme Court and Appellate Division statement of the jurisdictional failure by not naming the objectors does not apply to this court because there is no such rule in this court and because of this the state court did not deal with the constitutional issues.

11. The US Constitution protects under the 14th Amendment these petition signers and they should not be allowed in this case by the board of elections whereas they were not in the proceeding before the Board of Elections.

12. The State Board of Elections and the New York City Board of Elections are not just administrative bodies. They have executive and judicial functions which violate candidate's rights. These boards are selected by Chairmen of the Republican and Democratic parties and are prejudicial because of their judicial functions in throwing candidates off the ballot after a hearing, thus violating their due process rights to fair hearing before a fair trier of the facts. Avery v. Midland County 390 U.S. 474 (1968)

Dated: Bronx, New York
September 5, 2014

....

Neil Grimaldi, Petitioner
2860 Buhre Avenue, Suite 1E
Bronx, New York 10461
646-229-7974

UNITED STATES DISTRICT COURT
NORTHERN DISTRICT OF NEW YORK

SAM SLOAN; NEIL V. GRIMALDI;
NEREIDA NARVEAZ; VENIADA QUINONES;
MILLIE QUINONES; TIARA LAWRENCE; and
TRINA JACKSON,

Plaintiffs,

vs. 1:14-cv-01071 (MAD/CFH)

NEW YORK STATE BOARD OF ELECTIONS,
Commissioners Douglas A. Kellner, Andrew Spano,
James A. Walsh, Gregory P. Peterson; ERIC T.
SCHNEIDERMAN, as Attorney General of the
State of New York,

Defendants.

APPEARANCES: OF COUNSEL:

SAM SLOAN
2860 Buhre Avenue
Suite 1E
New York, New York 10461
Plaintiff *pro se*

NEIL V. GRIMALDI
2860 Buhre Avenue
Suite 1E
New York, New York 10461
Plaintiff *pro se*

NEREIDA NAREAZ
1815 Davidson
Bronx, New York 10453
Plaintiff *pro se*

VENIADA QUINONES
1815 Davidson
Bronx, New York 10453
Plaintiff *pro se*

MILLIE QUINONES
1921 Jerome Avenue
Bronx, New York 10453
Plaintiff *pro se*

TIARA LAWRENCE
1921 Jerome Avenue
Bronx, New York 10453
Plaintiff *pro se*

TRINA JACKSON

NEW YORK BOARD OF ELECTIONS
40 North Pearl Street
Suite 5
Albany, New York 12207

OFFICE OF THE NEW YORK STATE ATTORNEY GENERAL
Albany Office
The Capitol
Albany, New York 12224

Mae A. D'Agostino, U.S. District Judge:

MEMORANDUM-DECISION AND ORDER

I. INTRODUCTION

Plaintiffs commenced this action on August 29, 2014 and moved for a Order to Show Cause seeking injunctive relief "directing The New York State Board of Elections to place Sam Sloan on the ballot as a Democratic candidate for Government of New York State, Nenad Bach as Candidate for Lieutenant Governor of New York State, Geeta Rankoth as Candidate for Comptroller of New York State and Neil V. Grimaldi as Candidate for Attorney General of New York State in the Democratic Primary to be held on September 9, 2014." Dkt. No. 1 at ¶ 1.

Currently before the Court is Plaintiffs' motion for a preliminary injunction and Defendants' opposition thereto. *See* Dkt. Nos. 4 and 8.

II. BACKGROUND

The New York State Board of Elections received a designating petition purporting to designate Plaintiff Sam Sloan as a candidate of the Democratic Party for the office of Governor of the State of New York, Plaintiff Nenad Bach as a candidate of the Democratic Party for the office of Lieutenant Governor of the State of New York, Plaintiff Neil V. Grimaldi a candidate of the Democratic Party for the office of New York State Attorney General, and Plaintiff Geeta Rankoth a candidate of the Democratic Party for the office of New York State Comptroller. *See* Dkt. No. 8 at ¶ 3.

Subsequently, General Objections and Specifications of Objections were filed by three different objectors with respect to the petition for Plaintiff Grimaldi. *See id.* at ¶ 4. One objector stated that the candidate claimed 5,113 signatures and that the actual number of valid signatures was zero. *See id.* at ¶ 5. The second objector claimed that the petition contained 4,476 signatures, far short of the 15,000 needed. *See id.* at ¶ 6. The third objector claimed that the petition does not contain the minimum number of signatures required and fails to contain signatures from one half of the congressional districts in the state as required. *See id.* at ¶ 7.

Additionally, General Objections and Specifications of Objections were filed by two objectors with respect to the petition for Geeta Rankoth. *See id.* at ¶ 8. Both objectors claimed that the petition fails to contain the minimum number of signatures required, that the candidate does not meet the age requirement to hold the office, and that the candidate is not an enrolled member of the Democratic Party. *See id.* at ¶ 9.

On August 1, 2014, the Commissioners of the New York State Board of Elections met, at which time they determined that 4,087 signatures were filed and, therefore, the petition did not contain the 15,000 signatures required to secure the designations in question. *See id.* at ¶ 10. The Board of Elections also determined that Plaintiff Rankoth did not meet the age requirement to hold the office of New York State Comptroller. *See id.* at ¶ 11. By a unanimous vote, the Board of Elections found that the petitions for all four candidates were invalid. *See id.* at ¶ 12.

Thereafter, Plaintiff Grimaldi commenced a special proceeding in the New York State Supreme Court to validate the petition with respect to Sam Sloan, Nenad Bach and Geeta Rankoth, and to substitute another person for Geeta Rankoth. *See id.* at ¶ 13. The relief requested did not include an application to validate the petition with respect to Plaintiff Grimaldi. *See id.* at ¶ 14. The Supreme Court held a hearing on August 11, 2014 and Plaintiff Grimaldi sought to add himself as a party. *See id.* at ¶¶ 15-16. After the hearing, Plaintiff Grimaldi's request was rejected and, by decision order dated August 12, 2014, Judge Ceresia denied the requested relief. *See id.* at ¶¶ 16-17; *see also* Dkt. No. 8-2.

Thereafter, Plaintiffs appealed to the New York Supreme Court, Appellate Division, Third Department, which affirmed the trial court's decision. *See id.* at ¶¶ 18-19; *see also* Dkt. No. 8-3. In its decision, the Appellate Division cited to precedents from the New York Court of Appeals in addressing Plaintiffs' failure to name and serve the individuals who objected to Plaintiff Rankoth's petition and held that such a failure constitutes a jurisdictional defect. *See Sloan v. Kellner*, ___ N.Y.S. 2d ___, 2014 WL 4099330, *1 (3d Dep't 2014) (citations omitted). The Appellate Division also rejected Plaintiffs' argument that the State Board of Elections' composition is unconstitutional because it violates the Equal Protection Clause's requirement of "one person, one vote." *Id.* The court held that "the underlying principle of one vote per person does not apply to an appointive board, especially where it is charged with administrative duties." *Id.* (citing *Rosenthal v. Board of Educ. of Cent. School Dist. No. 3 of Town of Hempstead*, 497 F.2d 726, 729 (2d Cir. 1974); *Hadley v. Junior College Dist. of Metropolitan Kansas City*, 397 U.S. 50, 54 (1970); *Sailors v. Board of Educ. of County of Kent*, 387 U.S. 105, 111 (1967)) (other citation omitted). The court also rejected Plaintiffs' due process arguments and their argument that the designating petition signers' rights were violated by the Board of Elections' actions. *See id.* Finally, the Appellate Division held that the Supreme Court correctly determined that the State Board of Elections was free to perform a facial review of the petitions to determine if they are "in proper form and appear to bear the requisite number of signatures," which they did not. *See id.*

Plaintiffs sought leave to appeal to the New York Court of Appeals. Oral argument was heard on that application and, on August 27, 2014, the Court of Appeals denied leave to appeal. *See* Dkt. No. 8-4.

On August 29, 2014, Plaintiffs commenced this action pursuant to 42 U.S.C. § 1983, alleging violations of their First Amendment right to political association and Fourteenth Amendment right to due process and equal protection of law. *See* Dkt. No. 1.

III. DISCUSSION

Under the federal framework, injunctive relief is "an extraordinary remedy never awarded as of right." *Weinberger v. Romero–Barcelo*, 456 U.S. 305, 312 (1982). In the Second Circuit, a movant for injunctive relief must show "(a) irreparable harm and (b) either (1) likelihood of success on the merits or (2) sufficiently serious questions going to the merits to make them a fair ground for litigation and a balance of hardships tipping decidedly toward the party requesting the preliminary relief." *Blum v. Schlegel*, 18 F.3d 1005, 1010 (2d Cir. 1994) (citing *Jackson Dairy, Inc. v. H.P.Hood & Sons, Inc.*, 596 F.2d 70, 72 (2d Cir. 1970)).

"The *Rooker-Feldman* doctrine provides that the lower federal courts lack subject matter jurisdiction over a case if the exercise of jurisdiction over that case would result in the reversal or modification of a state court judgment." *Hachamovitch v. DeBuono*, 159 F.3d 687, 693 (2d Cir. 1998) (citation omitted). "Such jurisdiction is lacking because within the federal system, only the Supreme Court may review a state court judgment." *Id.*

In *Exxon Mobil*, the Supreme Court held that the *Rooker-Feldman* doctrine "is confined to cases of the kind from which the doctrine acquired its name: cases brought by state-court losers complaining of injuries caused by state-court judgments rendered before the district court proceeding commenced and inviting district court review and rejection of those judgments." *Exxon Mobile Corp. v. Saudi Basic Industries Corp.*, 544 U.S. 280, 284 (2005). In light of *Exxon Mobile*, the Second Circuit has held that "there are four 'requirements' that must be met before the *Rooker-Feldman* doctrine applies." *Green v. Mattingly*, 585 F.3d 97, 101 (2d Cir. 2009) (citation omitted).

> "First, the federal court plaintiff must have lost in state court. Second, the plaintiff must 'complain[ ] of injuries caused by [a] state-court judgment [.]' Third, the plaintiff must 'invite district court review and rejection of [that] judgment[ ].' Fourth, the state-court judgment must have been 'rendered before the district court proceedings commenced' - i.e., *Rooker-Feldman* has no application to federal-court suits proceeding in parallel with ongoing state-court litigation."

Green, 585 F.3d at 101 (quoting *Hoblock v. Albany County Bd. of Elections*, 422 F.3d 77, 85 (2d Cir. 2005)). "The first and fourth requirements 'may be loosely termed procedural,' while the second and third requirements 'may be termed substantive.'" *Id.*

In *Fischer v. Suffolk County Bd. of Elections*, No. 08–CV-4171, 2009 WL 2524859 (E.D.N.Y. Aug. 14, 2009), the plaintiff was a Democratic Party candidate for New York State Senate. *See id.* at *1. The plaintiff was not endorsed by the Democratic Party and instead sought to run by obtaining the requisite one thousand signatures from residents within his district. *See id.* After objections were filed, the Board of Elections determined that 620 of the signatures the plaintiff had obtained were invalid, leaving only 855 valid, which was short of the required 1,000. *See id.* Thereafter, the plaintiff initiated a proceeding in the New York State Supreme Court to validate his signatures. *See id.* The state court dismissed the proceeding on procedural grounds because the plaintiff failed to specify how the Board of Elections erred in invalidating the petition. *See id.* Further, the state court also sustained the Board of Elections' determination on substantive grounds, and found that it had properly invalidated a portion of the signatures. *See id.* After the Appellate Division affirmed the trial court's decision, the plaintiff brought suit in federal court seeking immediate injunctive relief to restore his name on the ballot for the upcoming election. *See id.* Denying injunctive relief and dismissing the complaint, the district court found that the suit was barred by the *Rooker-Feldman* doctrine and issue preclusion. *See id.* at *3-*4.

As in *Fischer*, in the present matter, the Court finds that Plaintiffs have failed to establish that they are likely to succeed on the merits. As discussed, Plaintiffs lost in state court and complain of injuries caused by a state court judgment. Additionally, Plaintiffs clearly invite the Court to review and reject the state court's judgment, which already rejected all of the arguments currently before the Court. Finally, Plaintiffs commenced this action after the New York Court of Appeals denied their application for leave to appeal. In fact, the attachments to Plaintiffs' motion for injunctive relief include the following: (1) the August 21, 2014 decision of the Appellate Division, Third Department; (2) Plaintiffs' reply brief submitted to the Supreme Court, Albany County; (3) Plaintiffs' "Letter and Motion for Leave to Appeal to the Court of Appeals;" (4) Plaintiffs' brief on appeal to the Appellate Division, Third Department; and (5) the Record on Appeal submitted to the Appellate Division. *See* Dkt. Nos. 4-1, 4-2, 4-3, 4-4, and 4-5.

Additionally, the Court finds that, even if the *Rooker-Feldman* doctrine did not apply to Plaintiffs' claims, the instant action would still be precluded by issue preclusion. The issue preclusion doctrine is properly invoked when a valid and final judgment has already determined a specific issue of law or fact. *Fischer*, 2009 WL 2524859, at *4. "Federal courts must give the same preclusive effect to a New York court's judgment that [state] courts would give it." *Wolff v. City of N.Y. Fin. Servs. Agency*, 939 F. Supp. 258, 264–65 (S.D.N.Y. 1996) (citing *Migra v.*

Warren City Sch. Dist., 465 U.S. 75, 83, 104 S. Ct. 892, 79 L. Ed. 2d 56 (1984)). New York courts apply the doctrine when (1) an issue was "necessarily decided in the prior proceeding and is decisive in the present action, and (2) the party against whom the estoppel is raised had a full and fair opportunity to litigate the issue in the prior proceeding." *Wolff*, 939 F. Supp. at 264–65 (citing *Murphy v. Gallagher*, 761 F.2d 878, 881 (2d Cir. 1985) (citations omitted)).

Here, all of the issues regarding the candidate Plaintiffs were clearly decided in the prior proceeding and Plaintiffs had a full and fair opportunity to litigate the issues in the state court proceedings. The Albany County Supreme Court and Appellate Divisions rejected all of the arguments Plaintiffs presented.

In their reply affirmation, Plaintiffs argue that this case involves the rights of five voters, who were not Plaintiffs in the state court case; and, therefore, the state court case *Rooker-Feldman* and issue preclusion cannot act to bar these claims. *See* Dkt. No. 9 at ¶ 2. Although Plaintiffs are correct that these doctrines do not apply to the claims of the non-candidate Plaintiffs, the outcome is the same. The information before the Court shows that Defendants complied with the Election Law in invalidating the petitions at issue. *See* N.Y. Elec. Law § 6-154. As such, all Plaintiffs, voters and candidates alike, have failed to state a cause of action under the Fourteenth Amendment. *See Thomas v. N.Y.C. Bd. of Elections*, 898 F. Supp. 2d 594, 599 (S.D.N.Y. 2012) (finding no due process violation for the voter plaintiffs when the Board of Elections complied with the state law and the candidates had the available judicial remedy under Article 16 of the Election Law) (citing *Rivera-Powell v. N.Y.C. Bd. of Elections*, 470 F.3d 458, 468 (2d Cir. 2006)). Additionally, to the extent that Plaintiffs are claiming that the Election Law at issue is unconstitutional, other courts have already upheld its constitutionality against similar challenges. *See, e.g., Queens County Republican Comm. ex rel. Maltese v. New York State Bd. of*

Elections, 222 F. Supp. 2d 341, 349-51 (E.D.N.Y. 2002) (finding that sections 6-154 and 16-102 did not violate the plaintiffs' rights under the First Amendment).

Based on the foregoing, the Court finds that Plaintiffs have failed to establish that they are likely to succeed on the merits of their claims; and, therefore, Plaintiffs' motion for injunctive relief is denied.

IV. CONCLUSION

After carefully reviewing the entire record in this matter, the parties' submissions and the applicable law, and for the above-stated reasons, the Court hereby

ORDERS that Plaintiffs' motion for injunctive relief is **DENIED**; and the Court further

ORDERS that the Clerk of the Court shall serve a copy of this Memorandum-Decision and Order on the parties in accordance with the Local Rules.

IT IS SO ORDERED.

Dated: September 8, 2014
Albany, New York

Mae A. D'Agostino
U.S. District Judge

paid $505.00
rec #ALB008

U.S. DISTRICT COURT
N.D. OF N.Y.
FILED
SEP 09 2014
LAWRENCE K. BAERMAN, CLERK
ALBANY

UNITED STATES DISTRICT COURT
for the
NORTHERN DISTRICT OF NEW YORK

SAM SLOAN; NEIL V. GRIMALDI; NEREIDA NARVEAZ; VENIADA QUINONES; MILLIE QUINONES; TIARA LAWRENCE; and TRINA JACKSON,,

Plaintiffs

v.

Case No. **1:14-cv-01071 (MAD/CFH)**

NEW YORK STATE BOARD OF ELECTIONS, Commissioners Douglas A. Kellner, Andrew Spano, James A. Walsh, Gregory P. Peterson; ERIC T. SCHNEIDERMAN, as Attorney General of the State of New York,

Defendant

NOTICE OF APPEAL

Notice is hereby given that Sam Sloan, Neil V. Grimaldi, Nereida Narveaz, Veniada Quinones, Millie Quinones, Tiara Lawrence and Trina Jackson, plaintiffs in the above named case , hereby appeal to the United States Court of Appeals for the Second Circuit from the order dated September 8, 2014 which denied Plaintiff's motion for injunctive relief restoring the names of Sam Sloan on the ballot as a Democratic candidate for Governor of New York State, Nenad Bach as Candidate for Lieutenant Governor of New York State, Geeta Rankoth as Candidate for Comptroller of New York State and Neil V. Grimaldi as Candidate for Attorney General of New York State in the Democratic Primary entered in this action on September 8, 2014.

Date: September 8, 2014

Neil Grimaldi

Neil Grimaldi
2860 Buhre Avenue, Suite 1E
Bronx, New York 10461
646-229-7974

Made in United States
Orlando, FL
04 November 2026

90204180R00109